The Gift of Reading

THE Gift
_of_ Reading

DAVID BOUCHARD
with Wendy Sutton, PhD

ORCA BOOK PUBLISHERS

National Library of Canada Cataloguing in Publication Data
Bouchard, Dave, 1952–
The gift of reading

Includes bibliographical references.
ISBN 1-55143-214-5

1. Children—Books and reading.   2. Reading—Parent participation.
I. Sutton, Wendy K.   II. Title.
LB1139.5.R43B68 2001   649'.58   C2001-910951-2

First published in the United States, 2001

Library of Congress Catalog Card Number: 2001092682

Orca Book Publishers gratefully acknowledges the support for our publishing
programs provided by the following agencies: The Government of Canada
through the Book Publishing Industry Development Program (BPIDP), The
Canada Council for the Arts, and the British Columbia Arts Council.

Cover design by Christine Toller
Cover photograph by Stan Funk
Printed and bound in Canada

IN CANADA:
Orca Book Publishers
PO Box 5626, Station B
Victoria, BC Canada
V8R 6S4

IN THE UNITED STATES:
Orca Book Publishers
PO Box 468
Custer, WA   USA
98240-0468

03 02 01 • 5 4 3 2

This book was printed by Friesens Printers on acid-free paper
that is 100% post-consumer recycled and processed chlorine free,
and printed with vegetable-based, low VOC inks.

For the Sally Benders and Anne Letains of the world.
For you and the other teacher librarians who are
out there carrying the torch!

That *The Gift of Reading* might serve you and your cause.

D.B.

For the many dedicated professionals with whom
I have worked over the years. You enrich the lives
of young people each day by sharing your love
of literature and reading!

W.K.S.

ACKNOWLEDGMENTS

Thank you, Wendy Sutton, for your invaluable participation in this project. Your knowledge, experience, thoughts and values have strengthened and enhanced the text more than I can say.

Thank you, Maggie de Vries, my friend and editor, for committing so much of your time and energy to such an important piece of my life. You are the one who collected and organized the material of my life and work, material that most would not have recognized as being the stuff of which books are made. Your vision and hard work have allowed me to express my passion in words on the page.

Thank you, Bob Tyrrell, for the idea of recording my message in this way. For over ten years now, I have been sharing these beliefs and these concerns with any who would listen and my message is not an easy sell. Thank you Bob, for recognizing the book behind all those speeches.

Thank you to the staff of Orca Books for your combined energies and team approach to this project and to all that you do. Your closeness and ability to share in everything you undertake are qualities that I treasure.

Thank you to the parents and educators who see themselves in these pages and are willing to accept what needs doing and then do it. And thank you to those unappreciated parents and educators who have been carrying the reading flag for so long.

To all the kids to whom, in those early years, I did not give the gift of reading, I would like to say I'm sorry. Kids, I just didn't know. I pray that over time someone in your lives has made a difference (the one that I should have made) and that you were given the gift of reading. If you were, you will not be able to help passing it on to your children and grandchildren.

To my wife, my everything, Vicki, thank you, Sweetheart. Thank you for listening to my thoughts on this project for so long. Thank you for coming to agree with me (on most of it). Thank you for your desire to protect me when I am confronted by those who are unable or unwilling to hear.

DAVID BOUCHARD

We don't need lists of rights and wrongs, tables of dos and don'ts:
we need books, time, and silence. "Thou shalt not" is soon forgotten,
but "Once upon a time" lasts forever.

PHILIP PULLMAN
Carnegie Medal acceptance speech

CONTENTS

PREFACE BY DAVID BOOTH

In our technologically-driven world of educational agendas, it is such a pleasure to read a book that celebrates the familiar and necessary ritual of bringing print literacy to children, of sharing the pleasures of literature and and the secrets of how it works with those who will benefit the most from our efforts — tomorrow's readers.

In their book *The Gift of Reading*, David Bouchard and Wendy Sutton have addressed all of those participants involved in the reading lives of our children — parents, teachers, librarians, principals, superintendents, departments of education, publishers and writers. Using their own experiences as parents, authors and educators, they have outlined passionately what it takes for children to become confident and independent readers, and they offer us helpful suggestions for creating literacy environments at home and in school, including suggestions for books to share.

Inculcating a love for reading and supporting the ability to read in children takes the whole community. David and Wendy urge us to begin when the children are small, sharing the heritage of out-loud rhymes with them, reading the picture books that ring with language and learning, singing and telling stories. Children will join the literacy club when they are willing volunteers, sitting alongside those who read with satisfaction and enjoyment, then joining in and bringing voice to all those strange markings on the page. And we must continue to nurture and encourage these young readers as they move into chapter books, novels, information books, poetry, magazines, references, computers, and all the other resources of our print-rich world.

The authors present a well-researched and carefully-thought-out rationale for giving youngsters reading strategies and activities that will support authentic literacy development rather than practice exercises that never seem to connect to the actual reading of significant text. They are strong advocates for those children having difficulty in becoming literate, and they recognize the need for careful and professional intervention, where the processes of reading and of coming to love books are not wiped out by unconnected and decontextualized drill.

I was especially pleased that this book carries us into secondary schools and universities, demonstrating the need for time and money spent on reading at every age and stage of life's education. The authors give us examples of effective "reading schools" that set priorities for literacy learning as a school-wide philosophy.

The personal stories of David and his son struck a strong chord in me. With the compassionate care and support of others, we can come to literacy in a thousand ways: we can read scripts or children's books or letters or newspapers or stories about learning to read. We can read the world.

Reading is both personal and social; we come to this ritual of learning because of our interactions with wise others who support us into independence. As a society, we need to ensure that there are opportunities for everyone inside the reading culture, not for a select few who conquer the complete canon, but for each of us who chooses freely what is wanted in a literate life.

The readers of this book will rejoice in the personal stories, the school victories, the parenting strengths, the supportive policies, the knowledgeable administrators, the authors who write for young people — the community composed of all of us who are part of the process of bringing together child and print, so that we can establish a world where thoughtful and mindful readers and writers continue to grow and reflect throughout their lives.

Professor David Booth
The Ontario Institute for Studies in Education
University of Toronto

INTRODUCTION

The Gift of Reading is not the first book on the subject of children and reading to hit the shelves in recent years. It is one of many. The quantity of writing on the subject of bringing together children and books indicates that much needs to be said and that many prominent people in the field care enough to do the saying. Too many children are not learning to read as well as they should. Too many children know how to read but won't. Too many children have not received the gift of reading.

On your bookstore and library shelves you will find books for parents and books for teachers. You will find books of lists, books of ideas, books of analysis and books based on studies. And you will find one book that draws all of these together: *The Gift of Reading: A Guide for Educators and Parents*. In this book, David Bouchard and Wendy Sutton speak to parents and teachers, and they speak directly to administrators, the people who have the most power to bring about change in the schools. They provide lists, ideas and analysis and they refer to studies, but most importantly, they speak directly to all adults who have children in their lives. They remind you, the reader, that you need to take responsibility for getting those children reading. Helping children learn to read and to love reading is not someone else's responsibility; it is yours!

For too long the responsibility for teaching and encouraging reading has been delegated to primary teachers and teacher librarians. Parents, family members, intermediate teachers, middle school teachers, secondary school teachers, school-based and district administrators and those who work for ministries or departments of education, you all must embrace your role as mentors for the children in your lives.

Not only must you start reading to children and listening to them read to you, but every one of you must start reading for your own pleasure. It has been said that "modeling is not one way of influencing people, it is the only way!" Let us all, every one of us, become the models that our children need in order to grow up as readers.

David Bouchard has developed a simple litmus test that he uses on teachers and administrators when he is on tour. He asks his audiences a question that can only be answered by someone who has read at least the first Harry Potter book. This test is easily adapted to whatever book is popular among children at any given time. However, Harry Potter is particularly effective right now because J.K. Rowling's books have become such a phenomenon that a great many children have read them — boys and girls both. David's test reveals that few teachers and administrators have read Harry Potter. In other words, it would seem that few educators in North America care enough about turning kids into readers to take the time to read what kids are reading, even when it is a book as popular and significant as Harry Potter. Many educators are out of touch. David is concerned about this. You should be concerned as well.

The authors of *The Gift of Reading* have between them vast experience with children and reading. David worked for sixteen years as a teacher and twelve as a principal. A father of three, he grew up a nonreader, but is now a prolific and award-winning children's author. Wendy has committed her working life to teaching and to children's and young adult literature. She spent the first part of her career in a variety of schools and teaching situations followed by twenty-eight years as a professor of language and literacy education at the University of British Columbia. There she was dedicated not only to teaching teachers how to get children reading but to ensuring that they learned of and introduced to their students the most beautiful, powerfully written books available.

Combining their voices and experience has been illuminating for both of them. The results of their collaboration are guaranteed to be illuminating for you too!

DAVID'S STORY:

HOW A NON-READER BECAME A CHAMPION OF LITERACY

chapter 1

DAVID'S STORY:

HOW A NON-READER BECAME A CHAMPION OF LITERACY

*Literacy is not for the fortunate few. It is the right of
EVERY child. Teaching children to read is not the
responsibility of a chosen few. It is the responsibility of
every teacher, every administrator and every parent.*
– DAVID BOUCHARD

I am a simple prairie boy who became a teacher, then a principal
and then a children's author. Along the way I learned some
important things about reading, about learning to read, and, at
least as important, about learning to love reading. But it was not
until my mid-twenties that a group of children first gave me the
gift of reading.

My message is in some ways contained in my journey, so I
would like to share parts of this journey with you. Something from
my book *If You're Not from the Prairie* seems like the place to begin.

My hair's mostly wind
My eyes filled with grit
My skin's white then brown

My lips chapped and split
I've lain on the prairie and heard grasses sigh
I've stared at the vast open bowl of the sky
I've seen all those castles and faces in clouds
My home is the prairie and for that I am proud.

~ಎ~

I was born in the small town of Quill Lake, Saskatchewan, in 1952. Thirty-six years earlier, in 1916, my paternal grandparents moved from Lac St. Jean in northern Quebec to St. Front in northern Saskatchewan, a prairie hamlet of fewer than two hundred people. My grandparents came with seventeen children. Try to imagine having seventeen children, let alone moving across three provinces with them! My mother's family is also rooted in Quebec. At the time of the 1837 Rebellions in Upper and Lower Canada, the Mercier clan made the trek into northern Montana.

My mother's family was one of many families that migrated south at the time of the rebellions. After a few generations south of the border, her family moved up to Saskatchewan. They spent several years in a small village called Ponteix before finally moving to Regina, which is where my mother met my father. Dad was in the army and looked awfully good in a uniform. Today, he is one of the best looking eighty-three-year-old men on Vancouver Island!

In 1954, our family moved to Gravelbourg, in southwest Saskatchewan, a small francophone community of sixteen hundred people. My parents chose Gravelbourg for its culture and its schools. The town boasted two fine Catholic schools: a reputable school run by nuns for my sister, Diane, three years my senior, and for me, College Mathieu, a private, French, Catholic school run by the priests of the Oblate Order. Gravelbourg was at that time inhabited primarily by French speaking Catholics and still boasts one of the finest cathedrals in western Canada. Our community was home to the province's only French radio station and had a tradition of exceptional hockey teams.

Before we moved, my dad was a farmer and a lumberjack. As did many northern farmers, he would farm during the summer and trek into the bush to log during the winter. Many people are not aware of the vast forests that make up Saskatchewan's north. My godfather, Adrien, my eldest son's namesake and the man to whom I dedicated my book *Voices from the Wild,* died in an accident in those same northern forests. My mother and father left the farm, enrolled in hairdressing courses in Regina and moved to Gravelbourg to open a side-by-side barbershop and hair salon.

My parents were hard-working and doted on my sister and me. We lived at the back of the shops. We had a small garden at the rear of the property and a double car garage behind that. We only had one car, but we had a two-car garage. Two doors from our home opened into the salons. The door between our house and the beauty parlor was in my bedroom. Women often opened my door to walk through to the kitchen or another part of the house. Every Saturday morning I woke to the sound of women chattering while my parents did their hair. From the time I was six or seven, I recognized this chatter as the signal to roll out of bed, pull myself together and pitch in. I removed curlers, swept the floors and, on occasion, washed a head or two of hair! Diane and I helped out. Ours was a family that worked together, but no one worked harder than our parents did; we always knew that they were working for us.

Nothing was too good for us kids. I had everything a prairie boy in the late fifties and early sixties could dream of: skates and hockey equipment, a three-speed bike, a cassette player and transistor radio, the best baseball glove in town, and toys. We had every possible kind of toy.

But there were few books in our house — nothing but a Bible, a few cookbooks and the daily newspaper. Never during my childhood do I recall owning a single children's book. Had I expressed an interest in reading, our home would have had a library to make anyone proud. But I never asked for a book and it never occurred to my parents to give me one.

So, the absence of books in my life was not due to a lack of love or a lack of resources, nor was it due to an unwillingness to give me what was best for me. Just as it is not for a lack of love that so many children are not read to or given books today. Our parents didn't read to us because they had not been read to as children — not by their parents, not by their teachers. My father was the fourteenth of seventeen children and my mother was the second of eleven. Her father died when she was twelve, leaving her to help my grandmother raise all those siblings. The reason why my parents were not read to as children is obvious: their parents had neither the time nor the energy to do so. My parents had never been read to, so it never occurred to them to read to us.

As I said, they were the best of parents. They taught me to believe in myself. They encouraged my sister and me to participate in all the activities available in our town. I played the piano. I performed in plays and sang in operettas. Yes, operettas. College Mathieu was an all boys' school. When we needed a bride and bridesmaids for a performance of the operetta *Trial by Jury*, boys whose voices had not yet changed were cast in the female roles. I was the bride! My strongest memory of that experience occurred when we took the play to Regina and I found myself needing to use the washroom. There I was, decked out in a bride's costume. I couldn't possibly go into the men's! So I used the women's. I vividly remember my discomfort as I carried on a conversation with a trusting old lady while we stood next to the door, drying our hands. Even if I wasn't learning to love stories through reading, I was learning about them through drama, and I was gathering a few of my own!

In addition to performing in plays, I played hockey, baseball, tennis and golf. My father often coached these events. When he wasn't coaching, he was always on the sidelines, cheering me on.

David, the hockey player.

David, the bride in a school operetta.

For my fifth birthday, Dad had a small, two-iron with a flat head custom built for me. It was the type that could be used for driving as well as for putting. I loved that club. For my eighth birthday, Dad bought me a set of women's wooden clubs that he cut down to my size. Nothing pleased my father more than spending time with me, his son.

Books were not part of our home. But the television was. The television served the same purpose then that it does today. It kept us amused when our parents were working the long hours the business required. I remember getting the first color television in our town and the thrill of discovering a smudge of red in an otherwise green screen. Although I was involved in many activities and often played alone or with friends, television became a big part of my home life. The shows that we watched included sports, cartoons and news — not much in the way of quality programming. In my house we played games, we sang songs, we made music, we watched television. We engaged in many activities that were active and creative and others that were less so. Every moment was filled with love. The one thing we didn't do was read. Surely school would correct that.

For me, it did not.

I started school at the age of four. Actually, I had just turned four when I found myself in kindergarten. In my first school memory I am sitting by a third floor window of the old brick school building watching my house burn to the ground. I remember a nun, a complete stranger, standing by my side. I hadn't been going to school for more than a month when a fire destroyed our hair dressing salons and our home. The school was notified and I was to spend the night there – with the nuns. They were kind enough to take me up to the third floor where we could all get a view. As I watched, the nun reassured me that my family was fine and that I would see them the next day. While our home was rebuilt, I lived at school and the rest of my family roomed with friends. The whole experience gave me bad dreams that stayed with me for a long time. To this day, I remain uncomfortable with being alone for too long. My agent has been instructed not to book me away from my wife, Vicki, and my home for more than "four sleeps" during any one tour.

I had been enrolled in the jardin d'enfance, the kindergarten, even though I was really a year too young to start school. Because of the nature of my parents' work, I had learned coping skills early. I was a big boy. I had been taught to behave and perform, at home and at school. Halfway through the year, because I was big and because I seemed to catch on quickly, I was transferred into grade one. I was still only four years old.

I was far too young. I was not ready for kindergarten. I was not ready for grade one. And I was not ready to learn to read. But no one at that time understood the concept of reading readiness, let alone the need to stay home next to Mom or Dad or another caring and nurturing adult. Society did not have a grip on the concept of readiness — school readiness or reading readiness. Even today, too many parents and teachers assume that because a child is a certain age or a certain size he or she should be ready to master reading or whatever else is deemed appropriate. My parents and my teachers assumed that since I had managed to get into school I should be ready for what school had to offer me.

My most vivid memories of those early years are not of school; they are of church. I remember the long hours spent singing, serving Mass, readying myself for my First Communion and my First Confession. All the while, I was learning to please. I looked the part of the ideal altar boy, the perfect choirboy and the model student. I looked the part and, being a good Catholic boy, I played it.

I played the part of the model student so well that everyone assumed I was learning right along with the rest of my class. But, since I had never been read stories at home and my teachers at school were not reading to us, and since so few children's books were available to us at school, none that I found appealing anyway, reading did not interest me. I could see no reason to learn to read, no purpose in my life that reading would serve. Furthermore, I had a short-term memory problem that I continue to struggle with today. No one had or has ever tested me so that I might come to understand the nature of the problem, but certain things that seemed easy and normal for my classmates, caused me unbelievable trouble. I can remember being embarrassed at not being able to recite the alphabet as an eleven-year-old going into grade eight.

My youngest son Etienne has similar memory issues, but his were diagnosed at an early age. That early labeling led to his teachers' tending to focus on his disability rather than on his strengths. But that's another story, one that I will tell in later chapters.

On occasion, I had to memorize short poems and I was able to manage that. But I struggled with many things that my class-mates mastered with ease. I could not learn the alphabet or longer poems. I kept my difficulties secret. What would it serve for any-one else to know? After all, I was a people pleaser, not a disappointer. I had a good wit about me and was able to accomplish a lot through rote learning. And I was able to read aloud. Many teachers as-sumed that I understood what I was reading and that I was read-ing on my own during my leisure time. They assumed wrong. I understood all right, but only for the short term. I could under-stand each sentence as I read it, so that I could read it aloud cor-rectly, but I could not remember what I had read a minute or more earlier. I could not hold the meaning. Time did improve matters, so that when I did eventually find myself enjoying reading aloud to my own students, I was able to retain the meaning of what I was reading. I had needed to learn in my own time, not according to a schedule mandated by others. Many years later that facility with reading aloud that I developed as a child would allow me to engage children and myself with a serendipitously well-chosen story, and from that moment I would begin to learn to love to read.

So there I was, too young to be in school, with a memory problem to boot.

My primary years came and went. I was an outgoing boy, al-ways anxious to raise my arm in class, to participate in anything and everything. I found pleasure in the accolades that came fast and often for a kind boy with a good voice, a shining smile and impeccable manners. I remember, a little later, the local doctor's wife telling my mother how pleased she would be if I were to ask her daughter to the school dance. I was that kind of boy.

People often wonder how a child can get through school with-out reading and without his or her inability to read being detected. For me it was not a problem. I developed excellent listening skills. I grew skilled at picking up innuendo, at listening between the lines, so to speak. I picked up on everything that was going on around me and translated these bits of information into answers of all sorts. Most exams were based on studies and discussions that had taken place in class. I stored enough information to draw intelligent conclusions without reading a word. Over time, I honed my skills to the degree that I could project answers to questions that had not been dealt with in class. True, I was often wrong, but more often my responses seemed credible. Perhaps teachers conjectured that I had read something with which they were unfamiliar.

For book reports, a common assignment over the years, I chose books I didn't think the teacher had read. Then I read the first and last pages and created my own story. Over and over teachers commented on what seemed to be a wonderful book. Over and over I steered them clear, declaring that I didn't think that it was their kind of story.

If I had been read to at home, I would have arrived at school with an understanding of the shape and the appeal of stories. If my teachers had read picture books to us at school and shared their illustrations, I am convinced that I would have developed an interest in reading. I would have learned predictive skills that might have helped me to compensate for my short-term memory problems. But, while I might wish that things had been different, I do value many things about my early education. I believe that I and others like me succeeded because we were given the scope needed to develop alternative skills. I succeeded because I was able to maintain my self-respect and my confidence. I never for one moment thought of myself as disabled or weak. I merely didn't read.

Had I been identified as a non-reader, things might have been different. I might have been forced to focus on the things I couldn't do. I might have spent hours feeling my confidence erode as I pored over the alphabet or page after page of exercises that I could not master. Instead, I found my own ways of coping with the hard stuff, and focused on the areas where I excelled. I am deeply thankful that I was able to succeed, after a fashion, in getting through a system that was not meant for me — that was not and is not meant for non-readers.

I am thankful that I was able finally to discover the beauty and magic of the written word — a beauty and magic that nothing in my schooling even hinted at. Few have become readers as late in life as I did. Yet I did, finally, receive the gift of reading. I received it, and continue to receive it every day from the thousands of children who have allowed me to learn to read by reading to them.

In high school it was more difficult to disguise my reading difficulties, but by that time my coping skills were at their peak. I will never fully understand, however, how I managed to pass provincial standard exams in chemistry, biology and physics. In *The Schools Our Children Deserve*, Alfie Kohn describes how difficult such exams are. He argues that our curriculum is broken down into unnatural groupings, making the workload for our high school students unrealistic — requiring as great a time investment, in some cases, as that required to obtain a professional degree. My success in those exams remains a mystery.

Through my years in school, I had favorite teachers as every child does. If only one of those teachers had looked closely enough at me to notice that I wasn't reading, or had at least shared his own love of books with the class, I might have discovered the pleasures of reading earlier. I would have jumped through burning hoops for my high school math teacher, Mr. L. I would even have read a book or two had he asked me to or had he suggested a title that was one of his personal favorites. But Mr. L. was a math teacher, not a literature teacher. It never occurred to him to mention books in class, nor did he ever give me the slightest inkling that he was himself a reader. And, of course, he may not have been.

University was easier than high school. There were no provincial or national norms, only the expectations of instructors who in the late 1960s tended to be often fairly liberal. I remember a psychology professor offering all of us As if we agreed to participate in an anti-bacterial-warfare sit-in in Sheffield, Alberta.

As was often the case at that time, and I expect still is, most
high school graduates who planned to continue their studies enrolled in whatever courses were offered at the university or college
closest to them. For me, the choices were art, business administration and education.

I liked people and believed that my people skills coupled with
my sensitivity would make me a good teacher. Having been in grade
one at the age of four, I entered university at fifteen. I began school
too early, finished school too early, and started university too early.
Always too early! In the sixties and seventies, we were allowed to
begin teaching with a two-year diploma: a Standard A Certificate.
Jobs were relatively hard to come by so most of us did the two years,
got working and finished our degrees at night and through the sum-
mers. We were advised to get jobs as soon as we could — before our
degrees made us too expensive to be hired easily. All told, it took me
nine years to complete my three degrees — a general arts degree, a
bachelor of education and a master's in educational administration.
So, by the ripe old age of eighteen, I was in the classroom teaching.
There I was, a non-reader, responsible for, among other things, teaching reading. My first teaching assignment was at St. John School in
Regina, teaching grades six, seven and eight where I spent several
years working with kids at that age level.

For the most part, I taught French, physical education and
music. However, in those early years, I did teach language arts,
mathematics and a few other subjects on which I had previously
honed my avoidance skills. I managed surprisingly well, considering, but was not doing justice to aspects of education that I would
come to learn were so very important, specifically, turning children into life-long readers.

About ten years after I started teaching, I was asked to cover for
a grade eight teacher who had taken ill. I had an hour with nothing
to do but read the class a book that he had left for me, *Skinnybones* by

Barbara Park, then just published. The task proved to be an easy one with unexpected and wonderful consequences. I found myself loving what I was reading. And my audience loved it too.

On that day, in front of that class, I began to discover the exciting world of literature. The process would take time, but it had begun. My students were kind and patient. They could see that something special was happening and allowed me all the time I needed to develop my skills as a reader. They allowed me to share my learning and excitement with them. They allowed me to get excited about new books, new authors and new worlds. Almost always, they came right along with me. Without realizing it, they were giving me the gift of reading as I was giving it to them. It was a rich exchange.

No one had taken me there. No one had modeled well enough to entice me to read. No one had instilled in me a love of reading. And here I had lucked onto a good book and a willing audience. At times I was so captivated by the story that I almost forgot the children were there. A miracle had occurred. I was reading and I was enjoying it!

Years passed. I learned to read for my students and for myself. I learned to love children's books. To this day, books for children continue to consume me. For ten years, I read and collected books and shared my love of reading, of books, of the written word. Then, ten years after I began reading, I learned that I could do a great deal more to bring children and books together.

It happened in the late eighties when I was vice-principal of a British Columbia secondary school. I was to oversee an alternative program for teens who were struggling in the regular system. I had come late to the world of children's books, but recent converts can be the best advocates! I went to my fifty-three fifteen to eighteen-year-olds and told them that I would be reading them children's stories once a week.

I told them that I had not been read to as a child and had only recently discovered the exciting world of children's literature. I expected that, by virtue of the fact that they were in this program, they were not unlike me. And sure enough, most of them had had limited experience with children's literature, either at home or at school.

Their program was located off campus. My plan was to go down to their building once or twice a week but always on Tuesday mornings. They gathered in a common room, a place where they could kick up their feet. I would bring in my pack of favorite books and they would sit back and listen, once a week, rain or shine, whether they wanted it or not.

Not surprisingly, their response to my proposal was less than enthusiastic. In fact, someone at the back of the room expressed his displeasure by swearing loudly. When I asked the student to own up, three arms shot up. The others may not actually have sworn, but they wished they had. Nevertheless, I began what was to become a sacred ritual. I started with my old favorite, *Skinnybones*, written for grades four and five. I read another book and then another.

I couldn't be sure what effect I was having, if any, until one day in December when I was home with a bad flu. Leif, an eighteen-year-old in my program, broke a cardinal rule and called me at home.

"YO — Mr. B?"

"Who is this?" I asked.

"It's me, Leif, Man!"

"Leif Man?"

"Come on, Mr. B! Leif — at school, Man!"

"Where did you get my phone number, Leif?" I asked.

It turned out that John, the program's head teacher, had given it to him.

"What do you want, Leif?" I asked, growing angrier by the second.

"Some of the kids ... Well, we were just wondering ... Like ... Are you coming down to read or what? It's Tuesday."

"I'M HOME SICK, LEIF!" I barked.

"What? Too sick to read?" my harasser persisted.

I did not go read to them. But I did not go back to sleep either. An eighteen-year-old had gone to the trouble of tracking down the vice-principal's number and calling him at home on behalf of a group of non-conforming kids. And the reason? They wanted me to come read them children's stories. I recognized the event for what it was: the first glimmer of a calling. A mission!

I analyzed my situation. I thought about the difficulties I faced in the secondary system, most notably the sacred quest in our schools for the highest possible grade point average. Our teachers were not willing to take time to discuss or focus on literature. They were too wrapped up in their subject areas, on taking full advantage of every moment of instruction time.

A middle school might offer me a better chance of making an impact. I put in for a transfer. And, in the middle school, I believe that I did make a difference, but I felt that I should be able to accomplish more and to do so more quickly. The following year I moved into the elementary system where I believed that I could do the most good. I spent the next eight years as an elementary school principal, doing everything I could to champion literacy, to bring good books into the hands of every teacher and every child — to bring parents, teachers and children together in a common cause.

I began writing specifically for those who I thought needed me most. And I began talking with parents, teachers and administrators—with anyone who would listen—about what I was learning. Today, I am no longer in the school system. I left in order to devote all of my time to writing and to sharing with a broader audience my thoughts on books and reading and children and literacy. *The Gift of Reading* takes that process one step farther. In the following chapters I explore the ways in which each person who is involved with children — parents and care-givers, teachers, administrators — can give a child the gift of reading.

FAMILIES, BOOKS AND READING

chapter 2

FAMILIES, BOOKS AND READING

A house without books is like a room without windows.
No man has a right to bring up children without
surrounding them with books ... Children learn to read
being in the presence of books.
– HEINRICH MANN, 1871 – 1950

As you will have realized by now, this book is as much about those who don't read as it is about those who cannot read. You will soon read my words to teachers about their responsibilities and to administrators about theirs, but it seems appropriate to begin at home, where children start out on their journey.

After all, no one has more influence on our children than do we, their parents, their caregivers and their extended families. What we need to be doing in our homes is not complicated; all it takes is time and commitment: the commitment to become readers ourselves, to read with our children, to create reading environments in our homes, and to provide our children with an abundance of good books. If we, the families, follow through on all of these, we will send our children off to school ready to learn to read and to be readers for life.

I have three children; the eldest is twenty-three and the youngest is three. I know what a challenge parenting can be today and I have experienced the joys that children can bring to their parents' lives. Over time I have come to several conclusions about how best to promote books and a love of reading in my home and how I as a parent can best support the work of the school.

My wife and I read with our daughter every day and have done so since before she was born. And I work to ensure that the television does not dominate our household. The challenges in North American homes are great, they are ongoing and they vary from home to home. Reading with our daughter every day is easier for us than it might be for a single parent, for example. However, I believe that reading at home is important enough that all parents and guardians need to find ways to incorporate it into their relationships with their children.

In homes in which English is not the first language, it is equally important that parents read to their children. By reading to them in their first language, parents are strengthening their children's concepts of language, reading and writing — of all the language abilities. For these children to be most successful in school and in learning to read and write in English, they need to have a strong grasp of their first language.

All parents, whether or not English is their first language, should also encourage their children to read to them. Reading to their parents or older siblings gives children opportunities to practice and to demonstrate their increasing skill and to receive positive reinforcement for the activity and the skill itself. Children love to have someone listen to them read, especially if that someone is supportive, enthusiastic and genuinely interested.

And why am I so convinced that reading aloud to children is the most important thing that you as a parent can do? Reading together at home is enjoyable and develops a sense of closeness and of sharing. Often family traditions are established as the stories shared become ones that your children in turn will read to their children.

Some Facts about Family Literacy

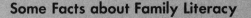

The literacy link between parent and child has to do with the role parents play in helping their children learn to read.

- Educational researchers have demonstrated that a child's progress in school is clearly related to his or her parents' literacy.

- Children raised in literate households are likely to enter grade one with several thousand hours of one-to-one pre-reading experience behind them.

- Research shows there is a better chance of a child becoming a fully literate adult if reading is encouraged in the home. Children who grow up where there are books and readers become readers.

- Family literacy programs are critical to the prevention of adult literacy problems.

- Children living with adults who have limited literacy skills, or in homes where reading and writing are not part of every-day life, are at risk of poor achievement in school.

from *Literacy BC Newsletter*, January 1999

Also, by reading to your children you contribute to their acquisition of language and reading skills, thus helping them become better equipped to begin their formal education. For example, as your children listen to you read aloud, they are being continually stretched as they hear vocabulary, language structures, topics and concepts that, through their own language and reading abilities, they otherwise may not encounter. It is also important that children not view reading as an activity they only do in school. When parents read aloud at home and share the pleasure books can give, they are also modeling reading, showing a valuing of reading, and demonstrating what it means to be a reader. Thus, by having and sharing in the reading experience, a child learns of the power and richness of language and of the rewards reading and literature offer.

If our children are having difficulty learning to read or are showing a limited interest in reading, we as parents need to seek ways of becoming involved. If we are going to combat illiteracy, we have to start at home. Two key areas need our attention. The television must not displace reading in our children's lives, or in our own for that matter. And we need to model a love of reading for our children, share the best books we can find, and provide our children with the tools they need to choose quality books for themselves.

An educational initiative in the U.S. called Start Early, Finish Strong provides a more detailed and far-reaching set of suggestions for parents:

> Hodges is also asking the parents of every South Carolina public school child to sign a new "Compact with Our Children" in 1999 and at the beginning of each subsequent school year. This pledge calls for teachers, parents, and students to share the responsibility for children's education and to live up to high standards. Parents pledge to:
>
> ★ Read to young children.
>
> ★ Encourage older children to read to themselves.
>
> ★ Provide a quiet, well-lit study area at home.
>
> ★ Ensure regular and punctual school attendance.
>
> ★ Provide adequate rest, food, and a healthy environment.
>
> ★ Support school activities by volunteering, visiting the classroom, and attending parent-teacher conferences.
>
> I would add to that list by suggesting that parents continue

reading to children even after they are able to read to themselves. Children are able to understand material read to them that is often too difficult for them to read. By reading more advanced stories aloud, parents expand their children's world and give them a taste of the rich reading material that awaits them as their own reading skills improve. Recognizing the fact that children's understanding of what they hear substantially surpasses their reading ability, teachers frequently choose books to read to their students that are about two years in advance of what children are able to read for themselves.

In many of our homes technology interferes with the creation of a good reading environment and with reading itself. Technology has become a vital part of how we relate to our loved ones. Many of our children have been watching television every day since before they could walk. To limit use of the television — to put technology into a new place in our homes — can be challenging.

In his book, *The Reading Solution: Making Your Child a Reader for Life*, Paul Kropp sets forth three guidelines for making our homes rich reading environments. He suggests that we rule the television, read with our children, and reach into our pockets.

Determining the role of the television and other technology is a critical step and modeling good reading practices is key to creating lifelong readers. Finally, children learn what we value, in part by observing our spending patterns. We should ensure that, where possible, those patterns reflect our belief in the importance of reading.

Parents, before we complain to our children's teachers or to their principal, we must be certain that we are doing our share. We are more important in our children's lives than any combination of educators. As a principal, I often felt frustrated when parents came to see me concerned that their child did not or could not read when I suspected that reading was not being modeled or encouraged in the child's home. Schools will be much more successful in teaching children to read when parents support and augment the efforts of the teacher and school.

In addition to being sure that you as parents are doing everything you can to promote reading in your own homes, you have a lot to offer in your children's schools as well. Even for the many parents who work outside the home, there are ways in which you can help free up time for the teacher to focus on the instructional needs of his or her pupils. Offering to be in the classroom for only one or two hours a week or less can make a significant difference.

Parents can help with many important but time-consuming tasks. For example, they can help put up classroom displays, tidy the classroom library, escort a child who needs to see the nurse or visiting specialist, and help youngsters get ready to leave for recess, lunch or at the end of a school day. Perhaps the most pleasant and rewarding activity is listening to a child practice reading as every child enjoys having a patient, supportive listener. Not only will the teacher be grateful for your assistance, but the children will enjoy having another adult in the class to whom they can show their work and talk about displays and other things in the classroom that they would like to share. Even though you are extremely busy, I am sure you would feel rewarded and find yourself looking forward to your time in the school and classroom.

Reading is more than an instructional program. Reading requires heart and soul, good modeling and an appropriate environment. Interest and cooperation from home are essential if we are to teach children to love reading. As a principal, I provided information for parents suggesting how they could participate in their children's development as readers. I also informed them of what we saw as the school's role in that process. Only through cooperation and communication can we hope to succeed in making reading an important part of every child's life.

For my purposes, I have expanded on Kropp's three guidelines. What follows is one of my weekly bulletins to parents, revised and updated.

Suggestions for Parents

If you have concerns that your children may be having trouble reading or may not be learning to love to read, here are a few areas that you might want to look at in your own homes. At the same time that you are addressing these areas, you may wish to speak to your child's teacher or to me, the principal. If we all work together, we are sure to be successful!

1. Rule the Television

A great detriment to your child's learning to read is overuse of the television and other technology such as computer games and Nintendo. Getting a grip on the electronic screen is essential if you are to create time and space for reading in your home. After all that has been said about the harmful effects of too much TV, many of our children continue to spend hours and hours perched there, in front of the tube (and this is without addressing the programs that they should not be watching!). Some families solve the problem by watching no television during the week — some have gone so far as to sell it. I have never come across a single person who has regretted either decision.

2. Read with Your Children

When children see their parents reading, they learn that reading is important. A parent modeling good reading practices is even more important than a teacher or administrator doing it. In addition to seeing you reading books of your own choosing for your own pleasure, your children should see you reading the same books that they are reading. If your teen loves a particular book, she or he will be thrilled to see you reading it and to have the opportunity to share thoughts and responses with you. Finally, but most importantly, you should build into your life a daily routine of reading with your children.

A few tips on reading with your child:

- read aloud to your child and do so on a regular basis
- read a wide variety of books, including picture books, novels, nonfiction, poetry, etc.
- involve your child in the choosing of those books
- suggest that your child read to you; take turns reading
- when your child reads aloud, do not correct his or her reading
- keep books in your car, in your purse, wherever you may have a few moments to share a story
- encourage your child to retell favorite stories
- ask your child to read aloud to you stories that he or she has written
- ask open-ended questions about those stories; show enthusiasm
- provide a special place for your child's books
- take your elementary school age child to the public library every week
- encourage your older child to frequent the public library as well

3. Reach into Your Pocket

At the same time that public libraries are an essential part of every child's life, there is something special about owning a book. It has been said that children should have access to five collections of books: their public library, their school library, their teacher's collection, their parents' collection and their own collection. It is never too early to start building that personal collection of books for and with your child. It need not contain many books, but they will be precious.

One way to gauge your family's spending on books is to compare that spending to your spending in other areas — technology or entertainment, for example. If you think nothing of spending fifty dollars on a video game or eighty dollars to take the family out for dinner and a movie, but balk at spending twenty dollars on a book that will last forever, perhaps a revisiting of priorities is in order. On the other hand, if money is very tight, hardcover books may need to be reserved for a rare treat — a gorgeous anthology of children's poetry for the whole family at the holidays, for example. Paperback books are usually reasonably priced and second-hand bookstores hold a wealth of opportunities.

And you can help by reaching into your pockets to support literacy in your child's school. With all the cutbacks that our schools are undergoing, they need funds from parents to help maintain and build school-based libraries. Financial support can be provided in several ways, such as through donations and fundraisers.

Above I have summarized my interpretation of the three R's identified by Paul Kropp. What follows is a more detailed exploration of my ideas on each subject.

PUTTING THE TELEVISION IN ITS PLACE

The author of *Charlotte's Web* predicted that television would have an enormous impact on our lives, but for good or for evil he could

I believe television is going to be the test of the modern world, and that in this new opportunity to see beyond the range of our vision we shall discover either a new and unbearable disturbance of the general peace or a saving radiance in the sky. We shall stand or fall by television — of that I am quite sure.

E.B. WHITE

not say. Each of us has our own opinion, of course, formed through our own experience. We also have the opportunity to influence what the nature of the impact of television on our lives will be.

Jim Trelease, one of North America's most dedicated professionals in the field of literacy, elaborates in *The Read-Aloud Handbook* on some of the ways in which television may interfere with child development.

★ *Television is the direct opposite of reading.* It requires and fosters a short attention span. Reading, on the other hand, requires and encourages a longer attention span.

★ *For young children television is an antisocial experience, while reading is a social experience.* The three-year-old sits passively in front of the screen, oblivious to what is going on around him.

★ *Television deprives the child of his most important learning tool: questions.* Children learn the most by questioning.

★ *Television interrupts the child's most important language lesson: family conversation.* Studies show the average kindergarten graduate has already seen nearly 6,000 hours of television and videos before entering first grade.

★ *Much of young children's television viewing is mindless watching, requiring little or no thinking.* (171-174)

Trelease's points do not mean that there is no place for television in our homes or that television can serve no useful or entertaining function in our or our children's lives. Instead he refers to a series of problems that arise from the indiscriminate use of TV, its overuse and its unsupervised use. His points stand to support the notion that we need to take a look at our TV and technology habits in order to assess how they affect the practice and enjoyment of reading in our homes.

Whatever we may think on the subject, the twenty-first century is going to witness ever-increasing developments in technology. We as parents and educators must strive to understand the advantages and pitfalls of technological advances, especially as they affect the lives of our children. While critics admit that neither the television nor the computer is harmful in itself, they provide strong evidence that the unguided, indiscriminate overuse of either can be detrimental to a child's learning and wellbeing. On the more positive side, studies have shown that children who watch a moderate amount of television perform in school just as effectively as those who watch none at all. In fact, educators have noticed dramatic increases in the language abilities of children ages three to five that appear to coincide with the advent of quality programs for preschoolers such as "Sesame Street" and "Mr. Rogers." A two-year study of PBS programming watched by five- and seven-year-olds indicated that viewing educational television had a positive effect upon children's reading ability while watching situation comedies and the like had a detrimental effect. These same researchers also found, however, that the biggest influence upon the children's reading achievements was the attitude of the parents toward books and reading. With the advent of captioned television programming, researchers found that students, particularly those for whom English is not a first language, made significant gains in reading comprehension and vocabulary development when instructed with television that was captioned.

In a study reported by Carolyn Abraham in the *Globe and Mail*, January 6, 2001, researchers found that IQs have risen steadily around the world over the last century. Even those skeptical of what such test scores actually indicate agree that more and more people are increasingly doing more complicated things. Although researchers cannot precisely say what is causing the phenomenon, they are convinced that the rise in test scores has been too rapid, especially in the second half of the twentieth century, for genetics or evolution to explain. Instead they claim that TV-watching and video-game-playing may be partly responsible for raising IQs and developing a new kind of visual literacy. According to Ulric Neisser, a Cornell University psychology professor and editor of *The Rising Curve*, the rapidly changing images of movies, television and video games have had a significant effect on the way people think. The big gains in IQ scores were not in areas such as vocabulary, factual information or arithmetic but in solving visual problems and answering questions creatively. Rather than replacing books and reading, it would appear that, if used wisely, television and computers can actually complement and extend a child's repertoire of learning skills.

Parents are pleased when their children beg them to buy them a book and such requests frequently happen after children have seen a film or video version of a well-written picture book or novel such as those televised by the PBS "Reading Rainbow" and "Wonderworks" series. *The Lion, the Witch, and the Wardrobe, The Hobbit, Sarah Plain and Tall, Where the Red Fern Grows*, and many, many picture books are just a sampling of the literature available on video or shown on TV. The movie of E.B. White's *Stuart Little*, filmed fifty-five years after it was written, led to a flurry of requests for the book at both libraries and bookstores. You can be sure that when the movie of Harry Potter becomes available, millions of new enthusiasts will clamor to read or have read to them the exploits of J.K. Rowling's popular young wizard. Clearly television has the power to inform and to entertain, but its benefits are most pronounced when parents and children view it together and share their thoughts and reactions.

While many families may experience a conflict between television and reading in their households, few take steps to improve the situation. In many cases, we adults share an obsession with TV that matches that of our children. Many of us have the TV on most of the time. As do our children, we use it to relax after a busy day, or to take a break between work and dinner or before heading out to work. We eat in front of the television. We encourage our children to watch TV in order to free ourselves to cook dinner, to get the laundry done or to sit down for five minutes with a cup of coffee. And, once we have developed the habit of sitting down in front of the noisy chatterbox, or encouraging our children to do so, we have lost the opportunity to relax in a quiet, peaceful environment where clarity of thought, good wholesome conversation or enjoying a good book is possible.

Many children arrive at school each day having already spent time in front of an electronic monitor, be it watching television, playing a video or computer game, or surfing the web. They often put in token hours at school so that they can hurry home to their televisions or computers. These same kids will often finish the night in front of a monitor of some form. Taken individually, each of these experiences with television or a computer may be perfectly valid. They can certainly provide entertainment and in many cases are educational. Taken together, however, they may leave the child with little time for other pursuits, including reading.

While speaking in Lethbridge, Alberta, I met a teacher who taught at a Hutterite colony who was substituting for a teacher on maternity leave. She had recently taken seventy-five books to school only to see them devoured by the children. They read her books over and over. They took them home. They treasured them. The same thing could certainly happen in any classroom. However, these children had the gift of time and the gift of quiet because Hutterite communities do not allow televisions in their homes. Even more impressive, these children had developed a love of reading. The rest of us are sometimes challenged to provide the same gifts to our children in homes with televisions or computers in almost every room.

~ා~

A house is not a
home unless it
contains food and
fire for the mind as
well as the body.

MARGARET FULLER

One thing to consider in shifting the emphasis away from television in our homes is the location of the television. Most of us have a television right in the middle of our most visible and busiest room — the living or family room. Not only does it become the most readily available form of entertainment, its prominent placement makes a statement about the priorities in the home.

When we walk into the Hockey Hall of Fame, we see sweaters, trophies and pictures concerned with hockey. Similarly, the home of a family who has spent the past fourteen years in Africa will communicate their interests, values and priorities. The walls will probably be covered with rugs, masks and artifacts. Then there are the homes where the emphasis is on books — where the walls are covered with bookshelves filled with books. Such homes give occupants and visitors alike a warm, cozy feeling. They speak to the interests and priorities of those families. On the other hand, a home that highlights a fifty-four inch television or a multi-media room such as might be found in the home of Bill Gates also makes a statement about priorities. Whatever is central and available in the home will be used — whether it is a television set or a wonderful library.

Just as it is important that we read with our children, it is important that we watch television with our children. We must be aware of what they are watching. We must teach them how to talk about and evaluate the shows they watch by commenting on and asking questions about them. To facilitate making TV watching a family activity, the television needs to be in a place where the family can gather comfortably. If the best spot for that is the family room, a cabinet that closes will give the TV less prominence. If another room is available, it may be a better choice.

I've talked with families who set time restrictions on all electronics in the home. They allow their children to watch television on certain days, for a predetermined number of hours. These parents are usually involved in choosing the programs that their children watch — remembering that children need to have input into such decisions, and increasingly more input as they grow older. These parents maintain a similar control on the time that their children spend in front of a computer. Most parents who exercise such vigilance find it best not to put televisions or computers in children's rooms. It is easier to keep an eye on when and what children are watching when the television and computers are more centrally located, but not dominating the environment.

Some families make it easier for everyone to resist the allure of the TV by dropping cable. In fact, I've talked to several parents who have done so and have never met one who was not pleased with the decision. No, I've not met one parent who talks about missing the warmth and comfort provided by the vast array of channels on cable TV. Yet the options available through cable are often too tempting to resist. With the number of channels available through cable today, any age of viewer can find something of interest to watch at any time of the day or night. Dropping cable but keeping the television set provides access to the news and programs such as "National Geographic" and David Suzuki's "The Nature of Things," as well as making possible the use of a VCR, an excellent tool for becoming selective in your family viewing.

LEARNING TO LOVE READING

Once television sets and computers are appropriately positioned in our homes and in our priorities, we will find ourselves freer to turn to books and reading. In *Let's Read About Finding Books They'll Love to Read*, Bernice Cullinan describes the importance of reading in the home:

> In the midst of a chaotic, topsy-turvy world, you can create an island of tranquility, free of commotion. Your children deserve it and so do you. Books and reading help to

~☜~

*It is a great thing to
start life with a
small number of
really good books
which are your very
own.*

SIR ARTHUR
CONAN DOYLE

slow the pace of life to a reasonable speed. Actually, books
and reading serve two purposes at home: They become
the reason for establishing a peaceful period and the means
for doing it at the same time. (10)

Let's take a look around our homes. Where are the books?
Parodying the words of Cuba Gooding, Jr. in his Oscar winning
performance in *Jerry Maguire*, "Show me the books!" Books can
and should be visible in our homes. I find bookshelves filled with
books, pictures, carvings, and small paintings very attractive. In
our home we have several and, in addition to serving the obvious
purpose of displaying our books, they are pleasing visual elements.

Likewise, children should have a place to display books in their
own rooms. They should have bookshelves to hold and highlight
the treasures that they have received from birth until the present.
They need a place to store that first book from Grandpa, or the
book that you gave them for their second birthday or the favorite
book from your own childhood that you have passed along. If you
can, add one chair per child and an extra one for you, or some big
cushions and a piece of carpet, along with a good reading light.
Make sure that each child has a good reading light beside his or
her bed as well. Most children love to read or to be read to in bed.
Do what you can to make the space warm and inviting. You could
go all out and wallpaper or paint a mural of a library on the walls
or you could simply put up a poster or two. The purpose is to
create a space where your children can retreat into books and where
you can join them for your daily shared reading.

In her 1971 Caldecott acceptance speech, Gail Haley discussed
the importance of interacting with our children, reading to them
and telling them stories.

Children who are not spoken to by live and responsive
adults will not learn to speak properly. Children who are

not answered will stop asking questions. They will become incurious. And children who are not told stories and who are not read to will have few reasons for wanting to learn to read.

If children are not read to at home by their parents or guardians, they will come to school lacking an understanding of the great gift reading can be in their lives.

Once we have got a grip on technology and have made our homes conducive to reading, the next step is to sit down and read ourselves and read with our children. The *Washington Post*, in "The No-Book Report: Skim It and Weep," May 14, 2001, deplored the fact that "a 1999 Gallup poll found that only seven percent of Americans were voracious readers, reading more than a book a week, while some fifty-nine percent said they had read fewer than ten books in the previous year ... The number of people who don't read at all, the poll concluded, has been rising for the past twenty years." The first step for parents, and for all adults, is to look to our own reading habits.

When I say we must read with our children, I am including a whole range of reading activities. First and foremost is reading aloud to our children on a daily basis. But listening to our children read aloud to us, both from published books and from their own writing, is enormously important. Also important is reading what they read. If you have noticed that your child loves Franklin, read Franklin books. If your child is into her tenth Goosebumps book, ask her to recommend one to you. Keep up with your children's reading through the years, even if you are no longer reading aloud to them — even if they are no longer interested in talking with you about their reading. It will mean a lot to them that you are interested and take the time to read their favorite books.

A Gift of Reading

DAVID: One of the artists with whom I have worked on picture books is Zhong-Yang Huang, whose paintings grace the pages of our Chinese Legend series. Yang and I have become close friends and on his last visit to the West Coast I wanted to give him a gift that meant a great deal to me. So I wrapped up a set of the Harry Potter books, presented them to him and suggested that he take them home to Regina to read aloud to his eight-year-old son, Sean. He was concerned that his difficulty with English would get in his way, but assured me that he would give it a try. Three weeks later he called to tell me that they were halfway through the first book and, though he struggled with his reading, he and his son were closer than they had ever been — that the experience was transforming and enriching their relationship. He called me on numerous occasions to update me on their reading. They have now completed the first three books and are headed into number four. Yang has told me that my gift to him is perhaps the most precious he has ever received. Books and reading are not only wonderful for their own sake — they are wonderful because of their transforming powers in the lives and relationships of the readers.

If your child has difficulty reading or shows little enthusiasm for books, your task will be greater and reading aloud to your child every day will be even more important. Make sure that you are choosing the best books available to demonstrate to your child the beauty and richness of written language. Look at the art in picture books together. Involve your child in the choosing of books. Make sure to keep up those weekly trips to the library and, if you can afford it, visit the children's bookstore regularly. If you don't have a children's bookstore in your community, ask your school or public librarian which bookstore has the best children's department.

Having spent the greater part of my life working with older students, I'm always surprised when groups whose focus is the very young call on me to speak. One such engagement came along a few years ago when I was invited to speak to the Daycare Givers of the North at the University of Northern British Columbia. I was anxious to ask the organizing committee why they had invited me. What could I possibly have said that would interest them enough to invite me? After all, I had never worked with nor written anything for three- or four-year-olds. It turns out that one of them had heard me saying that new parents should start reading to their children at the time of conception. Yes, that early and earlier! Ideally, reading aloud should start when a couple first discusses starting a family. Parents should not wait until their child can understand a story; they should not even wait for the birth of the child.

Your Baby Is Listening!

DAVID: As we all have, I had heard that babies can hear from within the womb, but not until recently did I come to believe. At forty-six, I was expecting my third child and was certain that my wife was carrying a girl. I talked to the baby as if she were a girl. I wrote to her as if she were a girl. And I sang the song "Daddy's Little Girl" to her daily. Three months after Victoria was born, Vicki was with her playing in the nursery. The house was noisy, but when I began singing "Daddy's Little Girl" in the next room Victoria turned her head aggressively in the direction of the song that I had not sung to her since her birth. The belief that a child can hear from within the womb is well founded. Parents, sing and read to your baby from the moment you know he or she is on the way!

It is never too soon to begin reading to a baby. Parents should read to their children every day from birth for many reasons, some of which are more obvious than others. The first reason and the easiest to appreciate is that reading to babies is a bonding activity. Reading aloud, singing lullabies and reciting nursery rhymes all promote sitting close to your baby, holding her and breathing into her face. In addition, the rhythm of language, the intonation of your voice and the variety and richness of the spoken word are all important to your baby's growth.

These same nursery rhymes, lullabies and stories offer many other advantages — ones more directly linked to a baby's developing language awareness — because they involve sounds, words, concepts and listening. Right from birth young children begin to respond to rhythm and rhyme. In no time being read to becomes a natural, enjoyable experience for them. Combining movements with rhymes and stories is also a fun way to introduce and reinforce words and concepts as you read aloud. Early childhood specialists tell us that the first twelve to eighteen months of a child's life is the time of most active development. During this period a baby discovers that sounds are words and that words have meaning. Thus, by being read to, babies begin to identify and recall specific words, books and stories, and their memory and understanding of these concepts are constantly strengthened.

As a result of daily exposure to books, a baby learns how to hold a book, where to begin reading a story, and even begins to understand the nature of print and its relationship to sounds. Through sharing stories in print with their parents, babies acquire a positive attitude toward books, and an understanding of how stories work and of the form and structure of written language. They begin to realize that pictures and words remain the same with each rereading and thus begin to recognize and recall the story or content and to acquire the related vocabulary. If the reader points casually to the words while reading, children will gradually

A Few Great Collections of Nursery Rhymes

- *Pat a Cake, and Other Play Rhymes*, compiled by Joanna Cole and Stephanie Calmenson. Illustrated by Alan Tiegreen.

- *Michael Foreman's Mother Goose*, selected and illustrated by Michael Foreman.

- *Rain, Rain, Go Away! A Book of Nursery Rhymes* by Jonathan Langley.

- *Over the Hills and Far Away: A Book of Nursery Rhymes* by Alan Marks.

- *Mother Hubbard's Cupboard: A Mother Goose Surprise Book* by Laura Rader.

- *Sing a Song of Mother Goose* by Barbara Reid.

- *The Real Mother Goose*, illustrated by Blanche Fisher Wright.

- *The Orchard Book of Nursery Rhymes*, compiled by Zena Sutherland. Illustrated by Faith Jaques.

learn that meaning is contained in those black marks on the page. Their aural and visual perceptions become sharper and will strengthen as their experience with books continues.

Babies' ability to understand is far in advance of their ability to express themselves. Even before one year of age, while still preverbal, a child can respond to a specific request by getting a book the parent has identified when asked, for example, "Bring me the puppy book." They also are able to point to a specific picture, and often the letter accompanying the picture, when requested to do so. By the age of two or three, toddlers are highly imaginative, and as their experience with books becomes broader and more varied, their vocabulary and understanding are also extended. They will begin sharing in the reading by pointing, repeating or filling in words, labeling objects, asking questions and confirming aspects of what they have heard — each an important developmental skill. By the age of three, children begin telling stories, retelling stories, and inventing stories, which will lead directly to early writing attempts and extend their oral responses to the written texts that are read to them. Adults working with young children are now aware that the language skills of listening, speaking, reading and writing develop concurrently rather then sequentially as was previously believed, with each skill informing and enhancing the others.

While the baby or toddler is absorbing the sounds and the words and the love, the parents are learning too. Their world is becoming a literary environment — one that they will not have to reorganize when their child reaches school years. Many parents do not start thinking about books until their children are at school and need help learning to read. All of a sudden parents realize that they need to make huge changes in their homes. By then, it is almost too late.

To promote reading-readiness and a love of books, new parents should begin by reading to their baby and should continue until their baby is old enough to read to them, at which time they will enjoy the fun of taking turns reading and asking questions. Parents, you will enjoy seeing and hearing your children discover the world of words, pictures and ideas. Likewise, they will always want more from you. They will want you to keep reading to and with them long after they have learned to read to themselves, and you should not stop — ever!

Another reason to begin reading children's books aloud before your child is born involves the honing of your skills. Reading aloud does not come naturally to everyone. Even those of you who are born performers can benefit from sharing stories with your partner, organizing and adding to your collection, setting new priorities

The Secret Magic of Books

WENDY: Many adults may be, as I am, just a little intimidated by toddlers. You can never be sure what their reaction to you will be. So, when I visit the homes of three much younger friends, I am relieved by the recognition and warm response that I receive from each of their one-to two-year-olds. My secret? I bring them books. As a result, as soon as one of those children sees me, she rushes to bring me a book. Sit down, her actions say, and read to me! The book may be one I have given, or it may not, but in the child's eyes I have become synonymous with books and reading. Even better, she has learned of the magic of books and is well on her way to becoming a lifelong reader.

and adapting your lifestyle to include daily sessions of reading aloud. If you are a novice, you might assume that because you can read to yourself you can pick up any children's book and read it effectively aloud. Not necessarily so! Children are discriminating listeners. Most teachers can tell you how they have worked at improving their reading aloud skills. If you have not honed your skills, your listeners might sit through one story, but don't wait around for them to ask you to read another. It could be a long wait!

One way to gain ideas and confidence for reading aloud is to take your child to the story times offered by most public libraries. Not only will you have an opportunity to learn of new books to share but you will also gather ideas of ways to read stories at home. For example, you will see how using hand puppets gives you an additional voice and adds to the pleasure for both you and your child when sharing a story.

A program of nightly reading requires a growing collection of books, or the building of a small collection and a regular pattern of visits to the local library. New parents should begin collecting these books well before the birth of their child. It can be a romantic process, putting together a collection of books that you will read to your child together, expecting that some day he or she will be reading these same books to your grandchildren. Finally, young

Reading (and Writing) to Your Child

DAVID: We began reading to our daughter Victoria three months before her conception; my wife and I read to her now at three years old, and, because she was a relatively late walker and talker, I anticipate that she will be a later reader. So, although we will read to her for many years to come no matter what her own skills are, our sharing of books with our daughter may be especially important. On Valentine's Day, six months to the day after her birth, I wrote her a poem in which, among other things, I talk about our commitment to reading to her and to telling her stories. Here is a snippet of that poem.

Victoria — this is our Love Story

This gift, I write for you ...

You're too young yet for cars or dolls.
You don't care much for most of your toys.
Your favorite thing (besides your mom)
Is listening to a story...
That we tell you every night at eight
A routine we've made sacred!
Thus a story dear — my gift to you
On this Valentine's Day ...

Writing to your child before and after her birth and throughout her childhood is a way of creating a lasting record of your love while showing her the value and meaning of writing as well as reading. It doesn't have to be poetry; a note, a story, anything you set down in print for your child is sure to be treasured forever. And your writing for her may inspire her to write stories or poems for you — something else to treasure!

parents should be reading to one another, or, for single parents, practicing on a good friend or family member. The practice allows you to discover the rhythm of language that is so important in all good reads and to develop your critical skills so that you can pick out the best books to share with your child. It also allows you to develop your own range of styles of delivery that will meet the characteristics of each book.

I strongly encourage parents expecting for the first time to develop a pattern of nightly reading aloud to one another, more than a pattern, a sacred ritual. If taking this step requires changes in television habits, so much the better! Parents will then be more prepared to model reading for their children. Through this nightly pattern, couples will find that their reading skills improve. For some the skills will come much more easily than for others, but everyone has the capacity to read aloud well.

When you read to a child, when you put a book in a child's hands, you are bringing that child news of the infinitely varied nature of life. You are an awakener.

PAULA FOX

An important part of this whole process involves choosing the right books. Parents must find books that they themselves find interesting — not just books that they believe will interest their baby at some later date, but books that truly interest them right now. It is difficult to put feeling into reading aloud a book you do not like. Parents will want to collect books on subject matter that interests them, in language that appeals to them and a presentation that works for them. If you have never had an interest in books for children, now is the time to start exploring, researching, trying books out, discarding them, trying others. Never has there been available such a wealth of wonderful books for children. You are in for a delightful surprise!

There was a time when the subjects of most books for babies and toddlers were limited to colors, the alphabet or baby's room. Today the choices are limitless! Whatever you choose to read aloud will give your baby your closeness and the soothing sound of written language. Making choices that celebrate the beauty of language, however, will help your baby learn to love language. It has now been documented that before birth your baby will become accustomed to the sound of your voice and to the sounds and rhythm of your language. Once he or she is born, the touch of your body and the smell of your breath will be added to these sensory experiences.

During the formative years, you as parents will play an important role in selecting stories to read to your children. At the same time you will quickly become aware which books your children seem to enjoy and respond to most. Once your child is old enough, you will no doubt find yourself having to deal with that endless refrain, "Read it again!" And if you are wise, you will concur while continuing to introduce new stories and to read aloud your own favorites. Many a parent has lost his or her taste for a particular story, at least temporarily, after reading it aloud three times a night for months on end. However, be assured that the repetition of a favorite story plays an important role in the developmental growth of your child. In addition to enjoying something that is familiar, a quality which is also important to most of us as adults, your child is strengthening his or her memory, vocabulary, and sequencing of words with each repetition of a requested story. Eventually the current favorite will lose its appeal and a new one will take its place. Young children will make their tastes known as they choose from the variety of books you have chosen. Later your choices may carry less weight, but for now get in there and provide your child with the very best children's literature available.

I have made frequent reference to the importance of sharing rhythmic and rhyming stories and poems with your baby or toddler. As your child gets a bit older, alphabet, color and counting books, and even board books, are excellent for sharing, but for the very early experiences, books that are rich with the sounds and rhythm of the language are particularly valuable and enjoyable for your baby. For this reason nursery rhymes and rhyming texts are always a perfect place to begin. Books that feature specific concepts such as colors, letters and numbers are more valuable a little later. Many collections and stories combine actions and simple tunes with rhythm and rhyme, which will greatly enhance the pleasure for you and your child and reinforce the sounds and meaning of the words. Linking rhymes with physical play when bathing the baby, "Rub-a-Dub-Dub," enjoying knee-ride games, "Pat-a-Cake," or naming face features and toes, "This little piggy," help babies learn words and word combinations with ease and pleasure. *The Baby's Game Book* by Isabel Wilner is an excellent collection of such rhymes. Actions come naturally when reading Patricia Hubbell's *Bouncing Time*, a fun-filled trip to the zoo that ends with:

> Then we'll wave a good-bye to the bouncity zoo.
> We'll bounce our way home. Bouncy me! Bouncy you!
> And after your supper and bath are all through,
> you'll bounce into bed — and I'll bounce in, too.

And then there is Sandra Boynton's *Barnyard Dance* with its square-dance rhythm and invitation:

> Bounce with the bunny! Strut with the duck!
> Spin with the chickens! Now Cluck, Cluck, Cluck!

Happily a wealth of wonderful books is available for the very young as they grow from babies to toddlers — books that will capture their attention and draw them back over and over again. In addition to the many collections of nursery rhymes that children continue to enjoy into their early school years, many beautiful color, alphabet and counting books in a variety of shapes and sizes, as well as board books and forms of paper engineering such as pop-up and lift-the-flap books, await the growing preschooler. Each offers a new way of viewing and responding to a book. An excellent example of a flap book is Jon Agee's *Flapsticks: Ten Ridiculous Rhymes with Flaps*. With each of the ten humorous rhymes, written in ABCA meter, is a picture representing the last word of the rhyme hidden under a flap, thus drawing the child into an imaginative and meaningful guessing game. Pop-up books, such as Chuck Murphy's *One to Ten: Pop-Up Surprises* and Audrey Wood's *The Napping House Wakes Up* never fail to please as, page by page, they reveal colorful animals and visual humor, and in the case of the latter, a cumulative story with a predictable, pleasing pattern. Nearly all of the rhymes and folktales popular with young children are available in board books, which are usually small in format and have pages that tiny fingers can grasp and turn. Also, it is never too soon to introduce young children to the rich diversity of the world's people by selecting from the many books that are available those that portray children of different ethnic and cultural backgrounds.

A Collection of Counting Books

- *Ten Go Tango* by Arthur Dorros. Pictures by Emily Arnold McCully.

- *One Lonely Sea Horse* by Saxton Freymann and Joost Elffers.

- *Circus 1-2-3* by Megan Halsey.

- *One Is a Mouse* by Jonathan and Lisa Hunt.

- *Twelve Ways to Get to Eleven* by Eve Merriam. Illustrated by Bernie Karlin.

- *Chuck Murphy's One to Ten Pop-Up Surprises!* by Chuck Murphy.

- *Ten Sly Piranhas: A Counting Story in Reverse (A Tale of Wickedness — and Worse!)* by William Wise. Illustrated by Victoria Chess.

Alphabet Books for All Ages

- *A Is for Asia* by Cynthia Chin-Lee. Illustrated by Yumi Heo.
- *The Accidental Zucchini: An Unexpected Alphabet* by Max Grover.

- *The Sweet and Sour Animal Book* by Langston Hughes. Illustrated by the Harlem School of the Arts.

- *Eh? to Zed: An ABeCedarium* by Kevin Major. Illustrated by Alan Daniel.

- *V for Vanishing: An Alphabet of Endangered Animals* by Patricia Mullins.

- *Trunks All Aboard: An Elephant ABC* by Barbara Nichol. Art by Sir William Cornelius Van Horne.

- *The Handmade Alphabet* by Lauren Ranken.

- *Into the A, B, Sea* by Deborah Lee Rose. Illustrated by Steve Jenkins.

- *The Butterfly Alphabet* by Kjell B. Sandved.

- *A Number of Animals* by Christopher Wormell.

Poring over lots and lots of books to choose favorites for you and your child can be enormous fun. It may feel a little daunting as well. You can get help from your local children's librarian, your children's bookstore proprietor and, once your child reaches school age, his or her teachers. Countless books can help you with lists and reviews of books that are right for you and your child. You might want to consult Michelle Landsberg's *Reading for the Love of It: Best Books for Young Readers* or Jim Trelease's *Read-Aloud Handbook* or perhaps *Long Ago and Far Away*, an encyclopedia of sources for intermediate readers by Otis Hurst. Keep in mind that all published lists of books will date; they are valuable for identifying older titles, but not for introducing you to more current books. To help with the latter, talk to the professionals mentioned above and watch the newspapers as well, especially leading up to Christmas, for reviews of the most recent books. Public libraries frequently develop lists of recommended books and current favorites among the various age groups. They also can provide access to quality reviewing journals such as *Horn Book, Booklist, Quill & Quire, and CM: Canadian Materials* to help guide your selections.

SUPPORTING YOUR CHILD AS A READER

Even though children in elementary school are learning to read, they need continual experience and challenge in order to progress. As you continue to read to them, they are hearing vocabulary, language patterns, ideas and concepts that will extend their reading ability because they are hearing written texts that their own reading skill would not allow them to read to themselves. At the same time they are experiencing the power and richness of written language and are being prepared to meet these more complex structures in their own reading and to use them in their writing. And, perhaps most importantly, they are gaining first hand knowledge of the value of reading and writing for their own pleasure and purposes.

As your children grow older, the issues around their reading will change and they will take a larger role in selecting their own books. Many parents become concerned when they see their children reading nothing but series books such as Arthur, The Magic Schoolbus and Franklin, also popular TV programs, or limiting themselves, as they grow older, to the Goosebumps, the Babysitter's Club, or the many horror series. Debates about the evils of formula fiction have been going on for decades. Think back to the Hardy Boys, Nancy Drew and Trixie Belden, books that first hit the stands in the early 1900s. Yet series books, specifically because they are written to a formula and offer predictable texts, have provided bridges into the world of literature for countless children. Children, and many adults for whom reading is a challenge, find safety in predictability — in knowing what to expect. Just as a small child may want to hear the same story over and over, so an older child may plow through twenty series books in a row, refusing to read anything else, simply because they are familiar and at his or her comfort level.

It is important that we, as adults, never disparage what children choose to read. Rather, note where your child's reading interests lie and try to introduce literature that is similar but will extend the quality of the reading experience. For example, if horror books by R.L. Stine are your child's choice of reading fare, introduce stories by John Bellairs, Susan Price, and Edgar Allan Poe, or some of the collections of "scary stories" by Patricia McKissack or Alvin Schwartz. Many teachers have capitalized on students' interest in Fighting Fantasies and Dungeons and Dragons by introducing them to the high fantasy of J.R.R. Tolkien, Susan Cooper, C.S. Lewis and Ursula LeGuin. Stephen Krashen, in *The Power of Reading: Insights from the Research*, uses extensive research to show that the use of light reading material, such as comics and teen romances, builds vocabulary and positive attitudes toward reading and can serve as a conduit to more serious materials. However, we cannot assume that the transition to better books will take place automatically. At this point parents and teachers have an important role to play. Perhaps the most serious limitation of the various forms of pulp fiction is that, in the same way that television displaces reading, they displace the wealth of literature that has the capacity to enrich young lives and transform children into lifelong readers. However, as implied by the suggestions above, a young reader needs the guidance of an understanding, caring adult in order to make the transition from formula fiction to quality literature. The most effective way to accomplish this shift is to read good books aloud to your children.

49

Children have more need of models than of critics!

CAROLYN COATS

Any book that helps a child to form a habit of reading, to make reading one of his deep and continuing needs, is good for him.

RICHARD
MCKENNA

Work to ensure, as has been suggested earlier, that you share in the whole range of your children's reading, whether you are reading these books aloud to your children or not. I have often had parents come to me, in my role as principal, complaining about a book or a series that their child's teacher, or I, had introduced or made available to the class. In order for us to talk meaningfully about the parents' concerns, they needed to have read the entire book. Many parents stop reading the books that their children are reading once their children reach grade four or have become competent readers. Few have actually sat down and read a Goosebumps or Babysitter's Club book from cover to cover. I would strongly suggest that you do so, not that you read series books aloud to your children, but that you become acquainted with and show an

Young People Love Sad Books

WENDY: Having English literature teachers as parents meant that books were an especially important feature of our home. The folk and fairy tales were often read to my brother and me, as were the stories of Beatrix Potter and Hans Christian Andersen, our favorite being "The Little Match Girl" — the tears would flow each time. We also loved Robert Louis Stevenson's *Child's Garden of Verses*, especially "The Land of Counterpane." My propensity for sad stories continued into my own reading with animal stories such as Eric Knight's *Lassie Come Home*, Anna Sewell's *Black Beauty*, and Marshall Saunders' *Beautiful Joe* heading the list.

Years later as a teacher, I realized that other eleven- and twelve-year-olds also enjoyed a good sob — I remember a student saying, "I want a book that makes me cry like Shannon has," when another girl in the class was in tears over a book. I had only to mention Marjorie Rawlings' *The Yearling* or Wilson Rawls' sentimental *Where the Red Fern Grows* to my university students to hear fond expressions of remembering and sorrow.

interest in what they choose to read.

In *Reading is More than Phonics*, Vera Goodman discusses the importance of children owning at least a few wonderful books. "Loving even ONE BOOK can influence a lifetime. Buy your children beautiful books. Take them to browse in the best bookstores in town. Some hardcover books will be expensive — but worth it!" I don't know exactly when it started, but it seems to me that at some point in recent years, we have become overly conscious of the cost of a book. Even when we can well afford it, many of us do not like to spend money on books. But, as I mentioned earlier, each child should have a library of his or her own, no matter how small. In fact, parents and grandparents should also have their own personal library of favorites — books that they will read over and over to the children they love. Children will come to associate those special books with the adult who shared them. It means a great deal to children to have a selection of books chosen by loved ones with personal inscriptions on the fly-leaves detailing the time and place of receiving and the identity of the giver. There is magic in owning books — placing them on a special shelf to be read again and again and again — passing them on to children and children's children in the years to come.

Eden Lipson, in the *Parent's Guide to the Best Books for Children*, describes book giving: "One of the pleasures of being a parent, grandparent, godparent or just an attentive adult to a child is helping to choose books. They make such wonderful gifts. Books cost more or less the same as toys, last much longer, and give endless pleasure"(xiii). And isn't it so? Books can touch our children deeply. They nourish the imagination, the creative thinking process, and contribute to a child's bank of nostalgic memories. Caldecott Medal winner Chris Van Allsburg said, "children can possess a book in a way they can never possess a video game, a TV show, or a Darth Vader doll. A book comes alive when they read it. They give it life themselves by understanding it." One of the most effective ways

A Book and a Bear

DAVID: Choosing a favorite book is a personal thing and one of a child's first steps toward independence. I bring my three-year-old daughter, Victoria, a "B & B" home after every trip (I have been making too many trips lately). Thus I help to guide her selections. However, among the books I bring she has her favorites. At the moment she reaches first for Sandra Boynton's *Barnyard Dance* and for Dr. Seuss' *The Cat in the Hat*, two books rich in rhythm and rhyme.

we can encourage children to love books is by giving them as gifts and teaching our children to treasure them. A child who has been nourished by literature becomes more imaginative and creative in his or her play.

On a related issue, I think that in order to create a strong literary environment, one that is rich in literature, we need to support independent bookstores. I am concerned about the increase in mega-bookstores at the expense of local bookstores. More and more small bookstores, with their knowledgeable personnel, are being forced to shut their doors as giant outlets take their business, even though the larger stores are often on the outskirts of town and rarely offer the cultural expertise necessary in the recommending of books. How unfortunate for so many North American communities! But we can combat this trend by supporting our local small bookstores. Doing so may mean paying a little more money, but it means saving on gas and stress. Shopping for books locally allows us to take advantage of the expertise of our local bookseller and gives our children the opportunity to be a part of their literary community.

The bookstores may be gradually moving farther and farther away, but the libraries are not. Your local public library, especially before your children reach school age, may well be your best source of books and information. As often as you wish, and without spending a penny, you and your children have the opportunity to take home the books that you choose together to read over and over again. Such library visits should take place at least once each week. Your child can get his or her own library card, thus gaining independence as a reader. And you can find out which books have the staying power in your household to be worth purchasing for your child's personal library. May I also recommend that while at the library you choose books for your own reading pleasure so that your children see that reading is an activity enjoyed by all ages.

In addition, if you have the resources, you might want to set up an account at your local bookstore when your child gets older. Arrange a system of prepayment. Choose an amount that you can afford and prepay this sum. Now your child is free to drop into the store, alone, with you or perhaps with a friend. She can browse independently, find a book that interests her, walk up to the front counter and say, "Please put this book on my bill, Mrs. Stockdill." Can you imagine the impact? If she finds reading a challenge, or has not shown much interest in books, choosing and buying books for herself can be transforming. If she already loves books, she will be taking a part in building her personal library and in developing her own tastes. When I was a school principal, a group of parents from our school initiated such a program with our local bookstore. What a success it was!

Parents whose children cannot or will not read often find themselves at their wits' end, jumping from fad to fad in the hopes of helping their child. We are all bombarded on a daily basis with offers of help in the form of reading programs, expensive tutors and alternative schools. I strongly suggest that before you buy into radical solutions such as the above, you consider the place of books and reading in your own home and devote time to reading with your child. Researchers come to the same conclusion over and over again. The strongest influence upon the reading development of children is not linked highly with socio-economic variables, educational background or IQ. The strongest influence on the reading development of children is directly related to the attitudes of parents toward reading and to whether reading, and reading to children, is a constant priority in the home.

In some cases you will need support from a special program designed to teach reading. But do not let that program displace the time that you spend reading with your child. Remember that the most important component in developing a love of reading in your children will be the time you spend reading for your own pleasure and reading with them.

Teachers, Students and Literacy

chapter 3

TEACHERS, STUDENTS AND LITERACY

*Teachers are expected to reach unattainable goals with
inadequate tools. The miracle is that at times they
accomplish this impossible task.*

— HAIM G. GINOTT

Teachers, whatever we may say about parents not reading with their children or children coming to school with little experience with books, we cannot ignore our own responsibility for teaching children to read. When all is said and done — when the first assembly is over and our students are nicely tucked into their desks — the responsibility is ours. If our students have poor literacy skills after twelve years with us, or if they dislike reading, it is partially our fault.

Rather than taking responsibility for inspiring and teaching children to read all the way from kindergarten to grade twelve, too many of us are delegating. We must rethink the notion that primary teachers, teacher librarians and learning assistance teachers are the only ones whose job it is to turn children into readers. The job belongs to all of us. Excessive emphasis on curriculum at the expense of providing adequate support for reading and writing has worked its way from high school down to grade four and in some cases even into primary classrooms. At the same time, teacher librarians are having their hours cut and cut again to the point where they can do only a fraction of what they used to do to promote reading in our schools and among our children.

Statistics indicate that out of every class roughly a third reads competently and voluntarily. This group of children reads naturally, often having come to school as readers. They become children who love to read. The second third of the class learns to read, and though they may not be voluntary readers, they can and do read when called upon. The final third does not or cannot read. This third group is a combination of many groups — the learning disabled, the slower learners, and those who would prefer to do just about anything rather than read.

In Ontario, at the time of this writing, twenty-nine percent of grade ten students failed a recent literacy test. Boys performed more poorly than girls and results in the writing portion of the test were even lower than those in the reading portion. Whatever we may think about such testing, these results are disturbing.

We teachers achieve what we can in the time that we are allotted. We do our best to meet the expectations of the public. We report to and work under the direction of administrators who we trust are communicating with and representing the wants and interests of parents. We want what is best for our students and work day and night to achieve success. Yet, despite all our efforts, too many of our students are functionally illiterate upon graduation. They can neither read nor write effectively and, therefore, are often prevented from realizing their full potential.

We must become more flexible, less focused on making our way through a mandated body of material and more focused on addressing the specific needs of each of our students. Above all else, we must start to read. Many of our secondary school graduates cannot or will not read and, therefore, are leaving school illiterate. In most cases, it is not that they can't read, but that they

Were You Read to as a Child?

WENDY: Sadly, my only memory of being read to in elementary school was in grade four when our teacher introduced us to P.L. Travers' *Mary Poppins*. I loved the surprising things that Mary Poppins did, all the while insisting that nothing extraordinary had happened. Her umbrella was undeniably magical and it was such fun to feel part of the laughing-gas tea party on the ceiling and to dance under a full moon at the zoo. As we listened, we shared a secret life with the four children under Mary Poppins' charge. I am glad to know that today so many more teachers read aloud to their students than did when I was a child. Young people remember nothing with more fondness than the books that have been read to them.

don't read. Teachers, until this situation is reversed, we are not serving children adequately and that means that we are not doing our job, nor is the ministry, nor are our school boards, nor is the vast majority of parents.

Helping children learn to love to read requires a clear focus and carefully formulated priorities. No one method is the right one. But the combined, on-going commitment of all parties involved in working with children is essential. We all have a role to play and we all should know our own roles and those played by others.

Literacy is not for the fortunate few. It is the right of every child. Teaching children to read is the responsibility of every teacher from kindergarten to grade twelve, every administrator and every parent. Every child has the right to learn to love to read. And there is no magic to making it happen.

The situation in too many of our homes and classrooms is bleak. To bring about change, we all must start reading and become involved in promoting literacy. That said, I am delighted to be able to acknowledge that some rewarding changes in reading instruction have taken place in the past decade or so. The most encouraging are evident in those classrooms today where children are truly excited about books and about reading. In such classrooms, even many of those who have difficulty reading appear to be aware of the pleasure that books offer and seem willing to persevere with the task of improving their reading skills. In some elementary schools, books are everywhere in most classrooms. Teachers read with children, children read together, and children experience the pleasure of reading silently to themselves. No matter what subject area or topic the class is exploring, the children are engaged with a rich variety of books. The classroom is brightly decorated with writing, pictures and models extending ideas and situations from their reading that the children have chosen to explore in personally pleasing ways. Reading instruction often includes a variety of groupings: whole class reading experiences, the teacher working with small groups and individuals, small groups sharing their responses to a novel they each have read, and children reading independently the literature they have selected for themselves. Some teachers and schools have adopted a child-centered approach to instruction and, aware that children need large blocks of uninterrupted time in which to learn, have greatly reduced the number of rigid time blocks and bells. Classrooms such as the ones I have described are typical of those reflecting the values and philosophy of whole language, which will be discussed in more detail later in this chapter.

But much still needs to be accomplished and many classrooms do not yet fit the model described above. Secondary schools often are not organized in a way that will help young people develop as readers. Too often English teachers, sometimes because they teach as they themselves were taught, have fallen into the trap of teaching literature as if it were a textbook, dissecting and analyzing every line. Nothing is destined to destroy a desire to read more quickly than this.

As esteemed British scholar Margaret Meek has stated many times, teachers must learn to "trust the text"; they must allow the author to engage and guide the reader to understanding it. Rather than interpreting each word and line of a piece of literature and following it with a test, teachers must help their students learn to probe a literary text for answers to their own questions. Only in this way can students become independent, effective, enthusiastic readers of literature.

Many successful intermediate and secondary English teachers begin a school year or term by having the class read the same novel or other selection of literature together. Then, after the students have read the complete text, the teachers demonstrate a variety of approaches to exploring and interpreting it. They follow this whole class experience by briefly introducing a number of novels that are then distributed, one to each group of four or five students. Each group reads the entire novel before they meet to share their personal responses, interpretations and questions. Together they then plan ways to share their reading and their study of the novel with their classmates, many of whom end up reading all of the novels read by the various groups.

Following the class and group readings, students are encouraged to read a literary text that is of personal interest and to decide how they will acquaint others in the class with what they have read. This approach, modeling by having the whole class share a reading, then having students practice working with literature in small groups, then freeing them to choose their own novels to read and share, is authentic and empowering. Approaches to the study of literature similar to the above are guaranteed to develop students who are enthusiastic, voluntary readers of literature.

SETTING BOUNDARIES

It's easy to say "no!" when there's a deeper "yes!" burning inside!

STEPHEN COVEY

Teachers, we have learned many things, but many of us have not learned to say, "no." "No! I can't do everything you ask of me and still focus on the literacy skills of reading and writing. No — I'm sorry, but I can't!" Too often we listen to the handful of parents who come lobbying with pet projects; we devote more and more time to ministry or school board initiatives. And there, for many of us, lies the basic weakness in our teaching program. We try to do too much and, in doing so, end up unable to do justice to what I view as our most important task — helping our children become effective, passionate, lifelong readers.

In addition to spreading ourselves too thin, many of us have lost our passion for reading, or we never loved reading in the first place. Unfortunately, books have become less and less a part of our personal and professional lives. Jim Trelease, author of *The Read-Aloud Handbook*, expresses concern that only about half of teachers read for pleasure. We teachers, just like the rest of the population,

---

Teachers, You Must Speak Out!

DAVID: When I was a principal, I sometimes asked more of the teachers in my school than they should have been expected to give if they were going to focus on literacy and love of reading. One year, I volunteered our school to pilot voice mail in the district. At that time, I knew that we had two new instructional packages to implement. I knew that teachers had yet another new reporting system to adjust to. I knew the high student/teacher ratios that they were contending with. With that knowledge, I should have known that too much was being asked of these professionals. I should have known better, but did not. Only by knowing their limits and making those limits clear to administrators can teachers protect themselves and their students.

tend to spend our time, money, and energy on other things.

And we often find ourselves in packed classrooms with too many students with too many varying needs. Our student/teacher ratio is often not fair to us or to our students. The situation is further aggravated by the fact that children vary greatly in their rate of intellectual development and learn at different rates and in different ways. In his 1959 book, *The Nongraded Elementary School,* one of his thirty books promoting educational reform, philosopher and researcher John Goodlad states that when children begin school, they may differ in mental age by three to four years and that this variation becomes greater as they progress through the grades. In fact, the range within a specific grade is considered to be equal to the grade itself; for example, the range of ability in a grade six classroom could be six years. Given these facts, confirmed by child development research, Goodlad continues to question whether it makes sense to organize and teach children by age and grade when the differences among them are so great. Again, supported by information such as the above, a child-centered, individualized approach to teaching, often referred to as a whole language approach, appears to be the most effective for meeting children's diverse learning needs. Even with so many children and such a range of abilities in our classrooms, we still must teach children to read, keep them loving reading through their school years, and send them out into the world equipped to benefit from the richness that books and literature have to offer.

During the primary years, teachers do spend most of their classroom time teaching reading, writing and numeracy. As all elementary school teachers know, language arts makes up between a third and half of the curriculum right through grade seven. However, often when children move from the primary into the intermediate grades, they experience a shift in emphasis: a shift from being taught to read and write to a greater emphasis on the content areas of the elementary curriculum. Our educational system is designed for those who become competent readers by the end of the primary grades. Yet, after years of experience in schools, I can assure you that many of our children have not acquired the basic reading skills by the end of grade three. In addition to implementing strategies to get children reading and loving it by the end of grade three, we might want to consider accepting the range of abilities and rates of learning that we find in our classrooms and extending into the intermediate grades the opportunities for learning to read.

By grade four, teachers appear to hope and assume that literacy will be acquired as a natural consequence of their students' working with written materials. Somehow, we have come to believe that if children are in a setting that requires them to read — that is a classroom that uses textbooks for the various subject areas — they also will be strengthening their reading skills. And further that if some children are not able to handle the demands of curriculum materials, their inability to read can no longer be the responsibility of the subject teacher. As a consequence, children who have not acquired the basic reading skills by the end of grade three or four are too often left to cope on their own as best they can. Results show, time and time again, that some children are moving through the grades without having acquired the reading skills necessary for them to succeed.

.That shift in focus to the content areas leaves many grade four children, and older students who haven't yet acquired the basic reading skills, or who are having trouble reading or do not like to read, with nowhere to turn. Yes, we'll provide them with remedial material and the weaker among them with learning assistance. But too often such students are allowed to fall farther and farther behind; for many the fall will not be broken until they graduate from secondary school or drop out of school altogether.

Those of us who are parents and educators of children who struggle with reading often find ourselves feeling helpless. We simply do not know where to turn for help. But in fact we are far from powerless. A change in attitude and the implementation of a few school- or district-wide strategies can bring about fundamental change not only for children who struggle with reading but for all children. Most importantly, we — parents, teachers and administrators — must work together.

When I was an elementary school principal, I sent home regular school bulletins in which I promoted reading at home and at school. Part of my mission was to provide parents with an understanding of our approach to reading at school, to give them a rough guide as to how they might promote reading in their homes, and to facilitate cooperation and support between parents, teachers and me, the principal. What follows is a bulletin that I provided early in the school year. It outlines the ways in which we promoted literacy in our school. Many of the strategies and programs listed here are explored more fully elsewhere in this book.

Every home, every city, and every community has a character

Ask anyone about the community of West Vancouver, B.C., and they will tell you what our community is perceived to be. Ask about the character of Calgary or Ottawa or Victoria and you will likely get a pretty good idea of what that city is all about. Simply ask to find out what kind of priorities a community or a city or a family has and you will hear: "That family is an outdoor family" or "These people are very busy and don't have much time for the kids" or "Those folks love their cars. They spend all their money and free time on cars." Much in the same way, schools have a certain character.

People say of us that we are a school that loves to read.

Our focus on books has come about naturally. Our teachers, parents, administrators and children all enjoy reading.

Visitors to our school often comment on what they observe:

We love to read.

And why is that so? It is because our school offers:

1. A library as beautiful and as functional as any elementary school library in Canada. A library equipped with every possible convenience including the ultimate in librarians (and numerous support parents) who will leave no page unturned to see that all children learn to love reading. Our library is the heartbeat of our school.

2. The principal's collection: You need only walk in the front door to observe the principal's interest in children's books. What you can't know just by looking is that he lends his books to children every day (and gets most of them back).

3. START: Our school-based, silent-reading program. At a set time every day, everyone in our school reads. The children, secretary, teaching assistants, teachers, custodians, volunteers to our school, administrators ... absolutely everyone reads. Our children learn that reading is a priority and, through START, are guaranteed a fair, quiet moment to learn to love the written word.

4. Our classroom libraries: The most obvious and the best person to model reading (other than parents, of course) is a child's teacher. An important tool for every teacher is a classroom collection to draw from. The teacher can then pull a book from his or her shelf and say, "Victoria, why don't you try this book from my collection? It's one of my favorites." Our parent advisory council has supported

this program by providing us with money to purchase books for individual classroom libraries.

5. Our professional guarantee: Teachers and administrators commit to making reading available to all children, not just the thirty-five percent who pick up anything and read on their own, but all children. We are constantly studying our children to guarantee that every child is reading to the best of his or her ability.

6. On-going miscellaneous programs include our annual pajama party, an opportunity to meet real, live authors and illustrators; annual book fairs (new and used); fund-raisers such as readathons; parent volunteers reading to children on a daily basis; our principal regularly reading to children, and more.

   We have developed a character that we are proud of. Over the next few weeks, through this written bulletin, I will describe what I see as the role of the various parties involved in this process — my role, the teachers' roles, your roles as parents, and the roles our students play in their own education.

Instead of turning to the Internet or to curriculum directives for a new approach or a new program to address the difficulties related to reading in your classroom, consider the following suggestions:

★ Model reading for your students.

★ Use a balanced/whole language approach. Shift your focus from working your way through various curricula to embracing reading and literature in your classrooms.

★ Know each of your students' reading abilities and feelings about reading. Teach to their strengths and to meet their needs.

★ Learn to say "no" and to get support when you need it. To do this, you will need to drop some of your non-academic responsibilities and clear time for yourselves and your students.

★ Learn to measure success meaningfully.

★ Extend all these strategies through secondary school.

I also encourage you to read my suggestions in the chapters addressed to parents and administrators. Of course you can plan and teach without involving the others, but for the best results teachers, parents and administrators need to work together.

MODELING READING

As teachers, we seem to feel that we do not have the time to read for fun. We spend our valuable hours, in and outside school, planning, teaching and marking. We have report cards to write, new curricula to implement, and challenging technology to master. And most of us have families and personal interests — though sometimes our families and friends appear to come second. We need to remind ourselves that we can only be vital in our teaching if we are vital people outside of school. However, because of the countless demands upon us, we have convinced ourselves that we do not have the time to familiarize ourselves with the world of children's literature — let alone to read the books once we have discovered them.

Yet, teachers, you have the power to change lives. Increase the time that you spend with literature. Let your students see you read. Talk to them about what you are reading — the kinds of books you enjoy. If you don't read now, start! Your students must see you as a reader. Take note of the children who appear to be non-readers and, after learning about some of their interests, lend them books from your personal classroom collection that you think would be of interest to them. You have the power, in Prescott's words, "to lure them into the wonderful world of the written word." Remember, "Someone has to show them the way." That someone is you. You cannot hope to light a fire in the hearts of your students if the fire does not burn in your own heart. In order to turn a child onto a book, you must first love it yourself.

Read in order to live.

GUSTAVE FLAUBERT

Some time ago I was speaking to a large group of educators on Vancouver Island in British Columbia. The first two Harry Potter books had been released. Harry had already been on the cover of *Time* magazine. I asked my audience how many educators in the hall had read Harry Potter. I was not all that surprised to learn that less than twenty percent of my audience had.

Think about what that means. Educators, people who have devoted their careers and their lives to teaching our youth, had not made the time or had the interest to read what may prove to be the most popular piece of literature written for children during our lifetime. And, while I do not want to get into an argument about the merits of Harry Potter, I will say that if we fail to take an interest in the books our students love most, we are missing an important opportunity to increase their interest in reading and literature.

Our public librarians and our teacher librarians are ready and eager to help. They can tell us about award-winning books, exciting new authors, and what our students are devouring with enthusiasm. These professionals are there to help us find books that we like so that we may, in turn, excite our students. Our librarians can put the books right into our hands but, once they have done so, we must put other things aside and begin to read. We must drop everything and read — not only to our classes or to a few students but for our own personal pleasure. If we are to instill the love of reading in our students, we, whether we are parents, administrators or teachers, must first come to love reading ourselves. And I stress that to demonstrate a love of reading is as important for intermediate and secondary teachers as it is for primary teachers.

Although reading and what one chooses to read are personal things, certain qualities do characterize "a good read," whether for yourself or for sharing with others. Good literature, be it fiction, poetry, nonfiction or drama, offers a richness of thought and experience that has the capacity to involve the reader totally. It has the power to make you care about the characters, to wonder at their strength, determination or weakness, to ask yourself what you would do if faced with a similar situation. Literature immerses you in language that is more sensitive and imaginative than the everyday language that normally surrounds you; it has the power to engage you emotionally and intellectually. "I couldn't put it down" or "I didn't want it to end" are sentiments often expressed by people who have enjoyed a well-written book — a book they are eager to recommend to fellow readers and are likely to reread for themselves. These same qualities characterize a well-written children's book. By immersing young readers in the imaginative world of literature, you nurture both their desire to read and their growing awareness of the creative potential of language. Carefully researched, well-written information books are also a valuable form of children's literature that, like fiction, have the capacity to capture children's imagination and to kindle a desire to learn more about a topic that has caught their interest.

It doesn't take much for teachers to model good reading practices. After all, children are watching our every move. If we read in front of them, they will notice! Yet over my long career in education I saw few teachers model good reading habits, unless during a school-wide, silent-reading program. Even something as simple as having a novel on our desk or in hand when heading for the staff room conveys a strong message about our attitude toward books and reading.

Most teachers work hard to achieve what they need to in a school day. Teachers are focused professionals. Whether all parents believe it or not, many teachers work up to twelve hours a day and take work home on weekends. Many feel guilty about relaxing with a book during their working day. They feel they must use every moment of their time at school to mark, plan or prepare for the next lesson. And, of course, teachers are just like the rest of us; their homes are as likely as anyone else's to be dominated by televisions and computers. Many teachers who have not made reading a part of their personal lives find themselves unequipped to model reading for children.

As a principal, I often found it a struggle to get teachers to relax and read during the school-based, silent-reading program. I had to remind them regularly of our commitment. Some would not have been able to name a single book they had read during a month's silent reading. They were not only frustrated at being asked to sit and read quietly when they could be doing so much else, but, in many cases, they did not know how. They did not know how to sit and read for pleasure. This situation is sad, and even sadder because it is so common.

Teachers care deeply about the literacy of their students yet often overlook their best resource for turning children on to reading — their own passion for books and reading. And modeling a passion for reading does not cease to be necessary once children reach grade four or grade eight or some other arbitrary point in their schooling. All teachers need to develop their love of reading and then to share it with their students. The sharing may take a different form in a grade eleven chemistry class from the form it takes in grade four language arts, but it should still be taking place.

A Selection of Nonfiction To Get You Started

- *The Lost Wreck of the Isis* by R.D. Ballard, well known for his *Exploring the Titanic*.
  In this book, rich with illustration and colored photographs, Ballard details the discovery of an ancient Roman ship.

- *A Short Walk around the Pyramids and through the World of Art* by Philip M. Isaacson.
  Describes the effects of light, form and color on art forms, architecture and the viewer. Insightful text; outstanding photographs and color reproductions.

- *Raoul Wallenberg: The Man Who Stopped Death* by Sharon Linnea.
  A fascinating account of the Swedish architect who worked in Budapest during the latter part of WWII to save Jewish people from death by the Nazis.

- *The Story of Canada* by Janet Lunn and Christopher Moore. Illustrated by Alan Daniel.
  The first illustrated comprehensive history of Canada for young people. Striking full-color paintings, photographs and maps; well written text enhanced by folktales, legends and songs.

- *Kenneth Lilly's Animals* by J. Pope.
  Sixty-two animals and their young depicted in large, full-color paintings. The habits and habitat of each; maps showing where they are found; tables of facts and figures. Appealing and informative.

- *Discovering the Iceman* by Shelley Tanaka. Illustrated by Laurie McGaw.
  Recreates the story and world of a 5,300-year-old mummy — the oldest, best-preserved human body ever found. Fascinating text; striking photographs and illustrations.

BUILDING A CLASSROOM COLLECTION

Just as every principal should have a library of treasured children's books, so too should teachers have personal libraries from which to lend personal favorites. All individuals associated with the education system should have a library, however small, at school, and at home for that matter, of favorite children's books or books they think would be of interest to the students with whom they associate. Each person — teacher, teaching assistant, secretary, custodian or superintendent — with whom I worked during my thirty-year career was at some time admired by a child. And every time a bond is formed between an adult and a child, the opportunity exists to turn that child on to reading. A child may never have a teacher who gets him or her excited about a book, but when the custodian tells about a favorite childhood story, the seed may finally be sown. All employees of the school board who have any contact with children should have an interest in literacy.

A room without books is like a body without a soul.

MARCUS T. CICERO

Using Your Influence

DAVID: Many, many years ago, I was a young, "with it" teacher: I was the staff advisor to the student council; I coached several seasons; I even had long hair! In my school, our industrial arts teacher was anything but "with it." He impressed me so little that at his retirement gathering I called him by the wrong name. Yet, when I walked by the industrial arts room every day, I found myself stepping over the same group of boys. They sat waiting for this teacher, hoping that he would show up and give them a minute or two of his time. That man had power in the lives of those kids — power that he could have used to encourage them to read. Not one of them looked up when I walked by. He was "the man!" He had a responsibility to those boys — a responsibility to reach out to them, to ask them about their lives and to make links that would draw them in to books and learning. He had a responsibility to make a difference in their lives.

Of all the libraries in a school, the classroom library is most important. Although it is important to maintain an open, vibrant school library, classroom libraries are essential for providing children with immediate access to books. And we have known this for a long time. Over thirty-five years ago, reliable studies found that children in classrooms containing literature collections read fifty percent more books than children in classrooms without such collections. The research findings revealed that the more immediate the access to books, the greater the recreational reading by students. A number of studies in the 1980s identified a strong, positive correlation between voluntary reading and comfortable, visually appealing library corners. Effective classroom library corners and collections were found to include areas large enough to accommodate five or six children at a time, five to eight books per child in the class, a feeling of privacy, and a wide variety of children's literature attractively displayed. However, these same studies established that without teachers introducing books and incorporating literature into their daily teaching these physical factors on their own did not engage children with books.

A few years ago, I went to our school's Parent Advisory Council (PAC) and explained that all teachers needed a collection of well-written, appealing books to share with their students. I explained that if a teacher is trying to build upon the specific interest of a child with a related book, he or she will be able to do so most effectively if the book is readily available to offer to the child. It's not enough for a teacher to say, "Johnny, go down to the library and see if it has my favorite book." How much better for the child to hear, "Johnny, how would you like to borrow this book? It is one of my favorites and I think you will enjoy it." He will expect to love the book, and love it he will! Schools need money to finance classroom libraries. Our PAC came through with three hundred dollars per classroom, as well as a separate sum for the principal, the vice-principal and something even more substantial for our librarian.

Our staff then decided to take one of our professional days to go book shopping. We went as a group; our goal was to find books for our classrooms that both we and our students would enjoy. Energy and excitement filled the store as teachers called out titles and authors, naming both old favorites and new discoveries. The experience was electrifying! When we were done, we went out for lunch and then headed back to school to read, to organize our libraries and to prepare to introduce the new books to our students. Getting their hands on new books excites students almost as much as the energy and enthusiasm of their own teacher. The two together are a winning combination.

The first thing the teachers did to prepare for our book-buying excursion was to review the titles and types of books that were currently in their individual classroom libraries. Do I have a variety of literary forms — picture books, novels, poetry, information books? Are the various literary genres represented — folk and fairy tales, fantasy, historical fiction, biography, realistic fiction, adventure, mystery and humorous stories? Is there an adequate range of reading difficulty in the collection? Do I need new fiction and nonfiction to support our on-going classroom projects and areas of study? Are there books that authentically reflect other cultures and peoples? Do I need additional books by my students' favorite authors and illustrators? Are there new books I should find out about that have been well received by students in other classes? We were all aware that each book purchased should make a distinct contribution to the existing classroom collection.

Some of the intermediate teachers designed an informal inventory with their students to help identify current interests and reading preferences within the class. By having children share movies and programs they liked, interests and hobbies they had, activities and sports they enjoyed, and the kind of books they liked to hear read aloud and to read for themselves, these teachers prepared themselves to choose books that they were confident would

Choosing a Variety of Written Texts

WENDY: One of the things I always felt important to emphasize with student teachers when talking about reading aloud to their classes was the value of choosing from a variety of written texts. A "rule of thumb" that seemed useful was that they share a minimum of three forms of writing each day — fiction in its many narrative forms and genres, poetry, and nonfiction such as biographies, news stories and information books. In addition to a variety of written forms, primary children need to experience both picture books and novels. With a picture book, they hear a complete story in one sitting, while with a novel they can anticipate the next portion of a longer book. Even the youngest children remember exactly where the previous day's reading ended and are eager to share what they think will happen next.

be welcome additions to their classroom libraries.

The following year, we asked the parents for more money, but this time, we asked for the money in September making it possible for teachers to shop throughout the year rather than be restricted to one session. Our teachers began running accounts at our local bookstore. If they shopped elsewhere, they brought the receipts in to be refunded from their accounts at school. That same year, our PAC came into our classrooms and built bookshelves to showcase our collections. In one room, one of our parents painted a spectacular reading corner around the shelves that had been mounted.

Classroom libraries are a must, but teachers need help building and maintaining these libraries and should receive funding for book purchases. If teachers cannot find support for their attempts to establish a substantial classroom library, they will need to make a special effort to supplement their personal teaching resources with books from the school and public libraries.

Even in schools where families are more strapped for money, parents and students are often willing to support activities to raise funds for school and classroom libraries by having bake sales, garage sales, selling raffle tickets, organizing walkathons, or canvassing the neighborhood for various forms of support. Visits to the school by local public librarians to introduce children to some of the wonderful library books available are also very successful.

USING A CHILD-CENTERED, HOLISTIC APPROACH

Any discussion about creating a rich literary environment and emphasizing the pleasures of reading assumes that teachers and parents have already given first priority to books and to reading for personal enjoyment. However, the debate over the best way of teaching, and of teaching reading, continues. If instruction is thought of as a philosophical continuum, whole language would be positioned at one end and text-based instruction at the other.

Whole language incorporates child-centered, literature-based approaches where the instructional materials used to teach reading and writing are a rich variety of trade books spanning the literary spectrum from fiction to information books. From their first day at school, children are immersed in an exciting environment of books and literary experiences with the teacher using these experiences to build upon and extend the reading abilities of each child.

The more traditional "back to basics" approach, on the other hand, views learning as the sequential acquisition of specific skills and uses a graded series of textbooks and ability groupings to teach reading. Underlying this approach to instruction is the unfortunate assumption that all children begin school with the same abilities and needs and that they learn in the same way — the only difference being that some children learn more slowly or quickly

~☉~

*Reading is not a
duty, and has
consequently no
business to be made
disagreeable.*

AUGUSTINE
BIRRELL

than others. This understanding of the learning process seems to justify using the same approach and materials with all children.

In schools today many teachers are using a combination of these two philosophical approaches, with the whole language philosophy informing their child-centered, literature-based approach to teaching, and skill-based strategies, such as teaching the letter-sound relationships or phonics, being introduced into reading instruction when appropriate. For teachers using this more balanced approach, ensuring that children learn to love reading is as important as ensuring that they learn to read.

Teachers and parents need to understand the philosophy underlying each of these approaches to teaching reading in order to feel confident that the strengths of each are being used by their children's teachers. Although I was trained as a secondary music and physical education teacher and then in educational administration, years of experience have convinced me of what works best. After years of teaching a range of ages and curricular areas and observing thousands being taught by others, I have concluded that the most effective classrooms are those in which teachers use a child-centered, holistic approach.

Whole language involves a holistic approach to everything that is done in the classroom. The education research tool, the *Thesaurus of ERIC Descriptions*, first used the term "whole language" in 1990, defining it as a "method of integrating language arts 'across the curriculum' that uses the real literature of various age groups and subject fields to promote literacy (i.e., reading, writing, speaking, listening as well as thinking skills)" (284). A more comprehensive and useful definition was published in the *Journal of Reading Behavior*, also in 1990. B.S. Bergeron did a content analysis of sixty-four articles published between 1979 and 1989 and concluded the following: "Whole language is a concept that embodies both a philosophy of language development as well as the instructional approaches embedded within and supportive of that philosophy.

This concept includes the use of real literature and writing in the context of meaningful, functional and cooperative experiences in order to develop in students motivation and interest in the process of learning" (22, 4, p. 319).

Also fundamental in a whole language classroom is the role of the child. With the teacher's guidance, children learn to initiate, plan, develop and assess their own learning, making learning personal and meaningful. In a supportive, stimulating environment, they are encouraged to "take risks" as they approach the challenges of reading, writing and thinking. For example, children are encouraged to write the words that best express their thoughts, inventing spellings if they need to, so that their focus remains on the ideas they are expressing rather than shifting at that moment to worry about spelling. Since the invented spellings are words they understand and have chosen to use for their own purposes, they add the correct spelling to their personal spelling lists for future reference. Learning in a whole language classroom is often collaborative and, in the context cited above, children will assist one another by quizzing each other on the words they are learning to spell.

As a principal, I purchased and gave to each of our staff a copy of Marlene Barron's tiny treasure *I Learn to Read and Write the Way I Learn to Talk*. Barron has worked as head of New York City's West Side Montessori School and is on the faculty of New York University. Barron tells us that New Zealand has virtually no illiteracy because their children learn to read by reading and to write by writing; that is, they read real books, not the synthetic language of basal readers, and write for real, communicative or expressive purposes. Barron describes the essence of whole language in a way that I hoped my teachers would understand and embrace:

Whole language is a way of looking at children and how they learn. It is an attitude, a set of beliefs about how children learn. Its principles and practices are firmly grounded in research from many fields: linguistics, language development, sociolinguistics, anthropology, psychology, and education. Whole language was not born of economic or political or "expedient" decisions on how to educate children, as so many of the curriculum directives of state legislatures have been.

What's more, whole language is a full-time program. It can't be done just a few hours a day. It's being with children in a way that flows through the whole curriculum, the classroom, the home — every school day and weekends too. Whole language is a part of everyday life. It can't be stuffed in a textbook or done between taking attendance and lunch.

Whole language isn't a book or a reading series or a course. It's not a set of "magical" materials. It's not a skills-driven approach to reading and writing. You won't find it on a worksheet or in a workbook or in those graded readers with their restricted vocabulary, stilted language, and fragmented learning. (9)

As Barron has stated, whole language is a way of viewing learning, a philosophy firmly rooted in related disciplines and research. Whole language programs reflect the belief that language is a naturally developing human activity. From the moment a baby responds to and utters sounds, language is being learned and used holistically to be differentiated and refined later, but always in natural, meaningful contexts. It is through language that learning takes place and therefore classrooms need to provide "real life" situations in which language is used for genuine purposes. Whole language teachers believe that all children can learn to think critically and creatively if immersed in a rich learning environment and given individual support.

To teach from a context that has meaning rather than from

the abstract of a single letter — one that often has different sounds depending on its placement within a word — makes sense to me and to many other educators. Unfortunately, many parents, and some teachers, still think that children should be taught as they themselves were taught, where learning began with an emphasis upon the sequential acquisition of specific language skills before attempting whole sentences and paragraphs. It is no surprise that I did not find reading pleasurable. For me there was no pleasure in poring over endless symbols and learning unreliable rules that meant little more than work followed by soul-destroying tests. Many of my generation were taught to read with a rigid emphasis on phonics; many of us failed. Some did learn to read, but chose not to. Call them reluctant readers or what you will — the end result is a society in which many people are functionally illiterate because they cannot or choose not to read.

In Orin Cochrane's *Questions and Answers about Whole Language,* Kittye Copeland, a reading instructor at Stephens College in Columbia, Missouri, quotes one of her college students who felt that traditional methods, with their over-emphasis on skills, had failed her.

I can count the number of books I have read in a lifetime on one hand. Where magazines and newspapers are concerned, I'd just glance at the pictures and read bits and pieces. I have reason to believe that my intolerable dislike for reading stems from my elementary school experiences ...

When I recall my first experiences with reading, I immediately recall reading groups. Beginning in first grade, I was neither in the highest, nor the lowest group, but somewhere in between. Six years old, and already I had a label placed on my back ... I cannot recall exact exercises from the skill book, but I can remember feeling very bored with the exercises, almost as if they had no meaning to

me, except that the teacher required me to complete them
… My hatred for reading became stronger every day. I got
to the point where I would answer the questions by simply locating the answers in the text, without reading or
understanding a word. Reading for me was just sounding
out words and trying to recall details and facts. (29-30)

This student, who was neither in the lowest nor in the highest
reading group, became a non-reader because reading for her had
been reduced to a series of exercises. Clearly, while in school, she had
never experienced the pleasure that reading and books have to offer.
Sadly, she speaks for thousands of other students and the dropout
and illiteracy rates seem to attest to what she has described.

Yet, the solution we are seeking does not lie only in how we
are teaching our kids to read. It lies in our attitudes toward reading. The changes we make must be direct and concrete in the classroom and more importantly, they must be universal changes that
affect everything we do — both in our homes and in our schools.

Attitudes aside, the debate between the advocates of a "back
to basics" approach and those supporting the tenets of whole language has been with us for many years. Vera Goodman, in *Reading
is More than Phonics*, quotes from her native Canadian Alberta Program of Studies for 1942:

Please teacher, don't teach the beginning reader to read
by the phonics method. This method is long out-of-date. It
is based on the idea that in reading, the reader moves his
eyes from one letter to the next, sounding out the word. A
good reader does not move his eyes in this way and no child
should have this bad habit fixed upon him. It makes his
reading slower in speed and poorer in comprehension. (16)

Yet, despite the fact that sixty years ago the weaknesses in a phonics-only approach were clearly understood, many teachers and parents today continue to place too much emphasis on phonics and basal readers at the expense of a literature-rich environment in which children are encouraged to read real books rather than synthetic texts.

Phonics does have a role to play; however, it is merely a tool, albeit an important one, and over-emphasizing it is confusing and misleading. It should never be used as the only method nor as the first approach when teaching children to read. Steven Bialostok, in *Raising Readers*, outlines three areas that are problematic when a phonics-first approach is used:

1. The English language is very complex. There are, for example, more than fifty ways of pronouncing the letter "a" depending on the letters before and after it. Sure, phonics makes sense to adults because we already know the words after seeing them so often. But for beginning readers, it is very confusing.

2. An overemphasis on phonics does not make sense. There is no meaningful context for children.

3. Children can easily lose the meaning and purpose of reading if they learn from a phonics-first emphasis. (42-43)

The phonics approach restricts children to working with sounds, letters, syllables and words rather than giving them access to complete, meaningful sentences. Too often they are trying to read without a context for the bits of language they are trying to process and understand.

Some of us have accepted that we need not subject our better readers to repetitive phonetic exercises when it is obvious that such children know the symbol-sound relationships. We keep the phonics program with its drills and exercises for those who are having trouble reading. Too often we single out our poor readers, take them from their classrooms, and subject them to worksheet after worksheet, test after test. We allow our better readers to enjoy the rich variety of books they choose for themselves while subjecting our weaker readers to basal readers and special programs — neither of which kindles a desire to read in the way that literature can. Such is the nature of many of our schools. We identify a child's weakness and focus only on that, often losing sight of the broader goal — teaching the child to read.

In some cases an overemphasis on phonics and worksheets has made its way into kindergarten classrooms. In *The Schools Our Kids Deserve*, Alfie Kohn describes this unfortunate trend.

> In many places, things are actually moving backwards. Take "the children's garden," which is the translation of Kindergarten. In many places, it has been turned into a first-grade readiness program, with whole-class, teacher-directed instruction, written assignments out of workbooks, and frequent grading. This is being done to five-year-olds despite the nearly unanimous view among early childhood specialists that it's a horrible idea.(7)

Children will not learn to love reading — in fact many will not learn to read at all — if the mechanics are forced on them and their reading ability is measured and judged before they have had a chance to enjoy stories.

TEACHING TO STUDENTS' STRENGTHS

Parents, one of your most important responsibilities is to ensure that your child is being taught by teachers who are building on his or her strengths. Priscilla Lynch, from Brick, New Jersey, suggests

that teaching based on a whole language philosophy allows us to
focus on the child and not on the material or curriculum. Yet sometimes we, as teachers, become too focused on the subject matter
we are teaching — often at the expense of those we are teaching.
Our entire educational system seems to be geared to covering and
testing a set curriculum. To put it bluntly, perhaps one of the reasons it has been so difficult to get teachers and schools to question
the validity of the traditional approach to education is that a textbook, skill- or curriculum-based approach to teaching tends to be
easier, and often less costly, than equipping and structuring a classroom to meet the individual learning needs of each child. With the
textbook serving as the curriculum, preparation time for the teacher
is reduced as the accompanying teacher's manual provides the di-
rections for instruction, the questions to ask — and even the answers! And we cannot discount the persuasive strength of tradition. Many parents and teachers are convinced that children should
be taught as they themselves were taught.

Lynch suggests, in Cochrane's *Questions and Answers about Whole
Language*, that educators have now learned to place more emphasis
on identifying the strengths and needs of the child within the context of the whole person.

*When teaching, light
a fire, don't fill a
bucket!*

DAN SNOW

> That change has taken time. Most of us were not trained
> to recognize children's successes and needs in context. We
> tested kids in isolation and taught to their failures. Now
> we're learning to focus on what they can do, and teach to
> their strengths. We are accepting their approximations of
> our demonstrations, rather than looking for exact right
> and wrong answers. We've recognized that all learning is
> a series of approximations. Mistakes are simply a sign that
> someone has tried something. We've stopped putting all
> our energies into correcting and controlling. (26-27)

Unfortunately, while I support Lynch's child-centered approach to education, it is not an approach that I have seen widely used. Over and over, I have seen children who were experiencing learning difficulties diagnostically tested and then drilled on an identified area of weakness for months or even years.

My son's experience contrasts with mine and reveals the dangers inherent in labeling children and focusing on weaknesses rather than building on strengths. No one identified my learning disability; I was allowed to learn to cope through my strengths — strengths that took me through three university degrees, a twenty-nine year career in education, sixteen published books and now, here, to you! My memories of school, though sometimes frustrating, are not the negative memories that my son describes. His teachers, both in elementary and high school, focused on his weakness and ignored his strengths. He and so many like him deserve better. Sadly, I do not think the system has changed much since my son left school.

My school experience could have been more rewarding if my teachers had known me better — if they had recognized my strengths, my imagination, creativity and enthusiasm — and deliberately created opportunities for me to use them. They could have taught me more effectively if they had identified my learning difficulties and found ways to help me overcome them in a meaningful way. Looking back I realize that what I needed most was to have been read to — to have been introduced to the wonderful world of literature and the pleasures to be found in reading. What I did not need was to be handed stacks of worksheets that focused on and consequently reinforced what I did not know or understand. Unfortunately, I didn't have teachers who were enthusiastic readers — teachers who encouraged their students to become readers by reading aloud daily, having classrooms rich with good books, and introducing literature into all areas of the curriculum. The difference between helping children to overcome their learning problems and concentrating upon their weaknesses may appear to be subtle but is, in fact, glaring.

As I am sure I have made apparent, I believe that a balanced whole language approach is much better than a phonics-first approach to teaching children how to read. However, let me stress that the key factor is that everyone work together. The changes that I have outlined — changes of attitude, focus and commitment — are universal and essential to achieve a level of literacy that we can be proud of and one that serves all our children, not just a gifted minority.

To serve all our children, we must know each and every child. Elementary and secondary school teachers must be aware of the reading habits of every child under their care, not just the strongest and the weakest readers but every child. Teachers have many demands on their time and energy, but literacy must remain an important priority in every classroom, from kindergarten to grade twelve.

Folk and Fairy Tales Are a Must

WENDY: A case study I carried out with a colleague made me keenly aware of the importance of primary teachers reading the traditional folk and fairy tales to their students. Within the study, four cultural language groups of grade one children were interviewed — Cantonese, Punjabi, Italian and Spanish. One of the findings that intrigued me most was the type of literature that these six-year-olds enjoyed hearing. Although their responses revealed a wide range of reading preferences, traditional literature, primarily folk and fairy tales, proved to be particularly popular with each group, with Cinderella, Snow White, Goldilocks and the Three Bears, The Three Billy Goats Gruff, and The Gingerbread Man being frequently mentioned as favorites. As the parent interviews revealed, these stories had usually only been heard in school — a finding that emphasizes the importance of teachers ensuring that these universal favorites become part of the literary experience of all of the children within their care.

If all teachers from elementary through secondary school do not maintain a focus on literacy, then disabled learners, non-gifted children and children who have trouble reading will make minimal progress once they move into the intermediate grades. In many North American schools, we identify children at risk, take them out of the classroom and subject them to fragmented language activities that have been shown not to help them. Instead, we should be making all classrooms into places where books and reading are promoted — places where all children can learn to love to read.

In theory, and in clearly structured arenas, identifying learning difficulties and taking steps to eradicate them is a valid approach. Report after report encourages us to do both — to identify and to support children with learning disabilities. The problem, however, is much the same as the problem that we have in teaching children to read: time and focus. Classroom teachers do not have the time or the energy to provide ongoing remediation for those children who need specialized help. They are not able to offer the kind of support that learning disabled children need, nor to support on a continuing basis the child who, although not disabled, finds reading difficult. Instead, a small percentage of children is identified as in need and a program is put in place that requires them to be pulled out of their classrooms — set apart. This tendency is particularly unfortunate if the classroom they leave offers a literature-rich environment.

Although the practice of removing children with learning difficulties from their classrooms continues in varying degrees today, it has been much reduced since the end of the 1970s when "mainstreaming" was introduced into most North American schools. The mainstreaming initiative led to students with special learning needs or disabilities being enrolled in regular classrooms rather than being taught in separate, special classes. This more inclusive approach to education has resulted in educators trained to teach children requiring specialized assistance now working with them in their own classrooms. Although the amount of time varies across schools and districts, mainstreamed children now spend all or part of their school day in regular classrooms. Clearly, a child-centered, whole-language approach to instruction with its focus on the individual is the most effective way to accommodate the vast range of learning needs and abilities characterizing today's classrooms and schools.

Many famous people, including some of the world's greatest scientists and artists, had learning disabilities. Albert Einstein, Leonardo da Vinci, and Hans Christian Andersen all achieved their success and made their contributions in spite of their handicaps. What would have happened to these individuals if, early in their school years, they had been identified as being "learning disabled" (LD)? Having a weakness identified and made the focus of instruction can actually undermine a child's confidence in his or her own strengths. However, some children whose weaknesses are undetected by the system, as Bill Martin, Jr.'s and mine were, often learn to cope and to be proud of and build on their strengths.

JoBeth Allen, an associate professor in the Department of Language Education at the University of Georgia, supports this position in Cochrane's *Questions and Answers about Whole Language*:

Since we feel that educational labels tend to create more risks than they reduce, we aren't studying "at risk students"; rather, we asked ourselves how whole language instruction might be particularly important for "the students we worry about most." We share some assumptions, based both on our readings and on our own observations and analyses: Children who "fail" in school have also been failed by the school. We want to create literate environments where students can take risks without risking failure. In such classrooms, all children are equal, not in what they already know, but in what they can learn. We suspected

that some of our children would have to relearn risk taking because of the failure they had already experienced as
learners.

Allen expands on the notion that non-readers who fail early
often fail to make it through the system. Either they make their
way through "with difficulty and reluctance" or they fail or drop out.

We had studied developmental stages, and "the gift of
time." We had also studied the statistics on retention and
drop-out rates: about half of students who have been retained once don't graduate from high school; nearly 90
percent of students who have been retained more than
once drop out of school. We felt that the gift of time should
be given every day. Every child should have time to read,
to write, to interact with peers, to extend a learning activity to its natural, rather than a pre-ordained, conclusion.
(53-54)

Many non-readers merely put in time. Yes, they learn. They
learn to hide. They learn to fabricate answers, stories and excuses.
And these kids are the first to learn the limits of their abilities, the
limitations and the magnitude of their disabilities! The sad truth
in this is that, had the strengths of so many of these kids been
recognized and extended before they were nine or ten years of age,
many may have been able to succeed in "the system," some with
flying colors.

As I mentioned earlier, my son is one of those children whose
strengths were ignored and weaknesses "worked on" for years. By
grade four, he had been identified as having a problem with his
short-range memory. He was labeled "severely learning disabled"
(SLD), a label that qualified him for supplementary remedial assistance. Until that time, he had been a confident, happy little boy

who loved school. Over the following eight years, he lost his confidence and began to dislike almost everything about school. Of course, he might have lost his confidence and love for school regardless. However, had some of the energy that was put into identifying and focusing on his weaknesses been directed toward building on his strengths, he may have had a better chance of learning to overcome his difficulties on his own, as I did.

Now in his twenties, my son is no longer limited by his disabilities. He is done with school! He does not read, and neither dares nor cares to spend another minute in a school where he might be asked to concentrate on his weaknesses. At the time of this writing, my son is enrolled in acting school and is represented by Vancouver's best acting agent.

Too often, unfortunately, the time chosen for children to leave the classroom for specialized reading assistance is the time when the teacher is reading aloud to the class or the children are engaged in independent silent reading. The children taken from the classroom are therefore missing out on the very activities that would best support their efforts to learn to read. If you, as teachers, take only one thing from this chapter, let it be this: reading is not for a select few; reading is for all children. Every child in your class, whatever his or her weaknesses or disabilities, needs to be present when you read to the class, when children read to themselves and when activities around reading take place. If some children in your class find reading difficult or balk at participating, you will need to work that much harder to find reading material that is appropriate for and appealing to them. You will need to enlist the support of the teacher librarian and the involvement of parents. But children with difficulties with reading should never find themselves in another room doing worksheets or even reading with a learning assistance teacher while the rest of their class is engaged in a rich, communal reading experience.

Teachers must always be on the lookout for new books. The

right book for each child is out there. Someone must make the effort to find that book and bring book and child together. You must always seek to discover the interests and abilities of your students and incorporate these into your instructional program. The stories children love can serve as bridges to other materials related to the school curriculum. Teachers, parents, librarians and administrators can all play a part in that process, working together, unified in their focus on each child's reading needs.

Primary teachers are, by and large, as I have suggested, fully engaged in the process of turning children into readers. Most primary teachers read to their classes every day and model good reading practices. They view their students as unique, whole people and, although aware of each child's needs, place special emphasis on the strengths of each. However, even at the primary level, teachers' freedom to do what is best for their students is under threat. We need to take care that demands for accountability do not result in excessive testing in our classrooms, that teacher librarians and libraries remain at the heart of our schools and supporting our reading programs, and that the public understands why we need to stay child-centered and positive.

SETTING AND MAINTAINING PRIORITIES

Next to parents, no one has as much influence on children as do teachers. Even when peer influences become paramount, teachers remain important figures in children's lives. What parents cannot do, however, is step back in blind trust, assuming that the job of teaching their children to read is going to be done. They cannot be overly confident and detached because their child's teacher may be in a precarious position and need their help.

I know first hand the demands that are made on teachers' time. During my twenty years of teaching I experienced the grueling workload, the increasing demands from administrators — including

new objectives, new curriculum, new programs — and new ex-
tra-curricular expectations. I also remember the demands that
parents made on my time. And I remember the endless planning, the marking, and all the in-betweens. Teachers, I am not
writing this book with the goal of increasing your workload; yet,
if you are unable to put aside some of the extra demands on your
time — both teaching time and non-teaching time — you will
have difficulty implementing change. An essential skill, and a
hard one to master, is the ability to say "no." You can only do so
much and no more. If you cannot say "no," find a caring principal who will say it on your behalf.

Parents, you must understand that your child's teacher cannot
call you at home to say, "I need you to become pro-active as my
principal has too many new objectives and programs for me to be
able to focus on what I know has to be done!" Your teacher can't
call with, "I need you to petition my principal or the superintendent directly. I have four special needs students in my class and no
support. I believe that I am entitled to at least one teacher assistant and I am having trouble getting that support. Without it, I
cannot spend the time doing what I have to do to get my students
reading." If teachers could, many would say to you, "Please become involved as you can say things to my employer that I cannot.
Furthermore, I need money for resources to do what needs to be
done and, again, I cannot come to you directly. I have tried taking
my requests through the proper channels but have been unsuc-
cessful." Parents, you need to support the efforts of your children's
teachers and to advocate openly on their behalf.

In the following principal's newsletter I outline what parents
should be able to expect of teachers.

To get what you want, STOP doing what isn't working!

DENNIS WEAVER

What you can expect of your classroom teachers

1. Teachers must try to monitor the reading patterns of every child in their classroom. Teachers must model good reading practices. Few people have the kind of influence over your children that their classroom teacher has. That children see their teacher reading at his or her desk, in the hallway, etc. ... is very important. Thus the significance of START (our school-based, silent-reading program).

2. Teachers must work at staying current! Teachers must provide time in their daily routine for reading — silent and aloud.

3. Teachers must establish a personal/classroom library that they can share with children at teachable moments.

    These are a few of the challenges that teachers face when it comes to that all-important priority of making our school one that truly loves to READ.

    We want to continue talking about books and reading. We want the subject to be on the lips of our community, our staff and of course, our children. In many ways, the expression, "You are what you think you are" applies to this. We are a school that loves to read.

These are some of the steps I took to insure that all our children learn to love the written word — to love reading and literature. Having been a reluctant reader who does not remember during my twelve years in school ever being shown the rich and endlessly varied world contained in books, my commitment to make the experience of to-day's children different from my own childhood experience is genuine.

ASSESSING SUCCESS

Few terms in education are as current and trendy as "accountability." Somewhere along the way, our true priorities got lost in the
shuffle — a shuffle that has introduced new programs, method-
ologies, technologies and philosophies. We seem to have forgotten
that literacy is the first priority and, many believe, our schools'
raison d'etre.

*The man who does
not read good books
has no advantage
over the man who
cannot read them.*

MARK TWAIN

Being held responsible and accountable for what we do is necessary and right. But when I speak of accountability, I do not refer
to standardized tests. Assessments that are limited to objective
measurement and testing have been shown to be unreliable and
reductionist. Provincial or state grade-wide testing places unpro-
ductive stress on both teachers and students and often redirects
the energies of both so that learning is jeopardized. Such tests also
usurp valuable school time that is better spent on instruction designed to meet the individual learning needs of children.

When I refer to our being accountable, I am not suggesting
that we fall into the trap of seeking and working toward "newer
and tougher standards." Alfie Kohn, in *The Schools Our Children
Deserve*, argues that, "Conventional methods of measuring success,
notably standardized tests, aren't merely uninformed about the
educational issues that matter: they prevent us from understanding what is really going on and what to do about it." He goes one
step further, with an amusing and thought-provoking suggestion:

All persons given to pious rhetoric about the need to "raise
standards" and produce "world-class academic performance for the twenty-first century" not only should be required to take these exams themselves but must agree to
have their scores published in the newspapers. (111)

Parents and those who represent parents have the right to know what we are doing and what the outcome of our actions is going to be even though subjective assessments are harder to obtain than scores from objective tests. Measuring attitude, frame of mind and what we hope will be "a lifelong love of reading" is not easy, but it can be done. As with any form of meaningful measurement, observing, talking, asking questions and listening carefully to the answers are good starting points. Once you have made reading a part of your own life and the lives of your students, encourage them to express their thoughts about their experience with literature and reading. They likely will respond with the same honesty as they used when describing their frustration and disappointment at not being able to read.

Many teachers, both elementary and secondary, begin the school year by having their students dictate or write a simple, personal statement about their own reading. They might include book titles, authors and illustrators they like, books that friends have enjoyed that they want to read, when they most enjoy reading and being read to, and so on. Observing your students' reading habits throughout the school year is also an excellent way to gain insight into their attitude and approach to reading. Do they select and read books voluntarily? Do they exhibit pleasure in sharing with others books that they have enjoyed? Do their writing and artwork reflect aspects of their reading? Do they ask questions about and reflect upon what they read? There is so much for you to learn by observing your students as they participate in a variety of literacy and literary activities — the knowledge that you gain will inform both your teaching and your assessment of your students' progress throughout the school year.

THE ROLE OF TEACHER LIBRARIANS AND LEARNING ASSISTANCE TEACHERS

We are expecting too much and the wrong things from our teacher librarians and our learning assistance teachers. We expect these two groups to complete the task begun by primary teachers — the task of turning children into readers — and we expect them to do it largely without the involvement of classroom teachers at the intermediate, middle school and secondary levels.

It baffles and horrifies me to see that now, when promoting literacy in our schools is so important, teacher librarians everywhere are fighting to maintain their jobs. And in most cases, they are losing the fight. The vast majority of these teachers love their work in spite of what is quickly becoming a case of professional abuse. They give their heart and soul every day, with shrinking budgets, little support and appreciation and no guarantee that their jobs will continue from year to year. I believe that the root of this growing problem lies in the fact that administrators do not read and do not understand the role and contribution of our teacher librarians.

Teacher librarians are not in our schools to work with hundreds of children. Their primary function is not to teach children how to read nor is it to provide teachers with planning time. Our librarians are there to excite us — administrators, teachers and parents. They are there to excite us and to provide us with the resources that we need so that we might excite our students about books. Our libraries are at the heart of our schools. Every school library needs a professional to stock it, to keep it running effectively and to bring it to life by continually adding to and deleting from a collection that must be vital and constantly changing. It must remain current and reflect the needs of the school.

Librarians must have the skills, the resources and the time to communicate with classroom teachers in such a way that they can come to know what teachers love and want and might care to know about. They then endeavor to find and make the appropriate material available. Librarians sit down and talk with individual teachers about programs and specific units that will require support. It is the responsibility of our librarians to make available the material teachers need to do what must be done in the classrooms.

Learning assistance teachers also have had their role in helping children learn to read greatly overextended. They should not be expected to do what is being asked of them. These professionals should not have groups of students dumped at their doors to be taught how to read. These teachers are there to support plans and initiatives that must be based in the classroom and guided by the classroom teacher. The situation as it too often stands — where learning assistance teachers are left on their own to lead groups of children through parallel programs rather than working with classroom teachers — leads to frustration and ineffective use of time for teachers and students alike.

PROMOTING LITERACY AMONG ADOLESCENTS

A large part of the problem of students leaving school weak in reading and writing is caused by literacy not being addressed by all teachers — particularly in the secondary grades. Teachers believe that their role is to teach their area of the curriculum. If a student is not able to read or write or shows no interest in doing so, that problem tends to be left unaddressed. Teachers either assume that their students have the necessary literacy skills or they rationalize that they do not have the time or expertise to deal with the literacy problems that students bring to their content courses.

Unfortunately too many teachers wear blinkers and do not see the whole picture; they do not recognize the breadth of their responsibilities as teachers. If they did, they would acknowledge that literacy is an essential part of their mandate as teachers, no matter what subject they teach. Although students depend on having teachers who are passionate and knowledgeable about their particular disciplines in the curriculum, secondary teachers need to remind themselves that they are teachers first and subject teachers second.

Every teacher has a handful of followers — kids who would go the distance for him or her. If these teachers are not modeling good reading practices and are not part of the force that encourages reading, if these teachers are not openly enthusiastic about books and reading with their students, if these teachers are not lending these kids books from their personal collections, they are missing important opportunities — in some cases perhaps the only chance a child may have to become excited about books. Parents, your child's teacher, even your child's grade eleven chemistry teacher, is duty-bound to find the time and energy necessary to become familiar with the reading interests of his or her students and to encourage them to become people who enjoy reading. I would like to make three concrete suggestions to secondary teachers. First, initiate a silent-reading program, either in your school or in your classroom. Second, make sure that your students see you reading for pleasure. Third, work at determining which children under your care have difficulty reading or are unenthusiastic about books and take steps to help and encourage them.

You don't have to burn books to destroy a culture. Just get people to stop reading them.

RAY BRADBURY

It is extremely important that teachers learn which of their students have difficulty reading. If they discover young people who cannot read, they must do what they have been trained to do: become imaginative and find some creative, constructive way to help those students learn to read. These steps are not being taken frequently enough in secondary schools. Secondary school teachers teach close to two hundred different students; knowing all of them well is impossible. However, for teachers to identify those students in their classes who are struggling because of weak literacy skills — particularly those over whom they have influence — is not difficult. It is not only possible; it is expected.

As I say, every teacher has students who look up to him or her, who would do anything he or she asked of them, including read a book. Why not start there, with those children? Teachers, you know who these kids are! Talk to them. Search out fiction, picture books even, as more and more picture books are published every year with appeal for teens that are related to the subject matter you teach. Introduce a topic or theme by reading a picture book aloud. Ignore the complaints that it's for kids and press on. You will be surprised at how quickly those moans change to cries for more! Introduce and lend books you think will interest your students or make sure that the books you recommend are available in the school library. Collaborate with your teacher librarian in creating wall and book displays related to specific topics of your curriculum. Design one or two assignments per term that allow students to draw on fiction as well as nonfiction for their research. Give them the chance to write historical fiction or science fiction or a story set in some other part of the world for an assignment. Be open to their ideas for bringing fiction into the science, math, history or geography classroom. Talk to the teacher librarian and other teachers to discover ways of integrating literature and reading into your curriculum. I regard the use of literature in secondary school as both a means and an end — a means toward higher levels of intellectual thought and insight and an end as an introduction to an enriching, pleasurable, lifelong activity.

Some of the Many Picture Books for Older Children and Teens

- *ZOOM* by Istvan Banyai.
  A wordless book that offers a fascinating experience with changes in perception.

- *Hansel and Gretel* from the Brothers Grimm. Illustrated by Anthony Browne.
  Effectively dramatizes the change and emotional impact illustrations have upon one's experience with a well-known story.

- ***Rondo in C*** by Paul Fleischman. Illustrated by Janet Wentworth.
  Offers a visual example of an alternate narrative structure with many perspectives focused on one moment in time.

- ***Rose Blanche*** by Roberto Innocenti.
  Fixed historically in WWII. The authoritative, anonymous voice and photo-like style of the exceptional illustrations present a powerful political statement.

- ***Black and White*** written and illustrated by David Macaulay.
  Visually presenting four narrative strands simultaneously, this book illustrates many of the strategies associated with metafictive postmodern literature.

- ***The Stinky Cheese Man*** by Jon Scieszka and Lane Smith.
  A fun-filled, chaotic example of metafiction. The title page, introduction and stories burst their traditional boundaries and emerge as characters.

- ***Hiroshima No Pika*** written and illustrated by Toshi Maruki and ***My Hiroshima*** written and illustrated by Junko Morimoto.
  Each has been used successfully to introduce John Hersey's novel ***Hiroshima***.

- ***The True Story of the 3 Little Pigs!*** by A. Wolf as told to Jon Scieszka. Illustrated by Lane Smith. And ***Trail of Stones*** by Gwen Strauss. Illustrated by Anthony Browne.
  Both offer fine examples of alternate points of view, the latter in poetry.

- ***Faithful Elephants: A True Story of Animals, People and War*** by Yukio Tsuchiya. Illustrated by Ted Lewin.
  This true story of the bombing of Tokyo during the last stages of WWII emotionally dramatizes one of the tragic consequences of war.

When I'm invited into a secondary school to speak to teachers, I'm always confronted with questions such as, "And what of numeracy? Is it not as important as literacy?" Or "How can you honestly expect me to talk and think about reading when I have so much to cover of my own curriculum in such little time?" Or "All right then, give me strategies and suggestions as to how I can fit literacy into my subject area — be it social studies, science or mathematics!" To these teachers I say, to begin with, you don't need strategies or tools; you need a change of attitude. You need to stand back and look at the whole child before you. You have to make his or her wellbeing your concern! And let there be no doubt: your students do want to learn to read and in order to achieve their potential they need to be able to read.

However, as secondary teachers, you have a responsibility in addition to promoting and incorporating literature into your par-

The Languages of the Disciplines

WENDY: When presenting workshops with secondary school teachers as part of a school district's language project, I was delighted with the interest and response that I received from the teachers in the subject areas such as math and science. They began to realize why many students receiving remedial reading assistance were still not able to cope with the reading demands of the textbooks in the various subjects. One of the math teachers, who had previously taught in an elementary school, spoke of how he now understood why his younger students had been able to handle problems presented in a numerical form but had difficulty when the same problem was presented in the form of a narrative. A number of the teachers candidly admitted that they had not given any consideration to the language structures of their particular discipline when planning their courses and appeared to be genuinely interested in incorporating that aspect of their subject area into their teaching.

ticular area of study. You are the teachers best equipped to recognize and teach the language structures of your particular teaching subject. Each subject area or discipline views the world from a different vantage point and encompasses concepts, generalizations and procedures of investigation related to that perspective. Over the years vocabulary and language structures specific to each discipline have evolved and are constantly changing as scholars study, explain and reflect upon phenomena in terms of their specialized point of view. The natural scientist's approach is mainly one of describing, classifying, analyzing and attempting to explain observed phenomena. He or she therefore draws upon the language structures of his or her discipline to describe observations and guide analysis. History teachers, on the other hand, often use narrative structures and the past tense when teaching the content of their subject.

Secondary school students cannot possibly learn all the content of physics or biology, for example, but they can learn how to think and work in the various disciplines by being taught how knowledge in each subject is structured and expressed. This recognition of the importance of the language structures of a discipline has led to a dramatic shift in the teaching of mathematics. Math teachers have become aware of the importance of preparing mathematically literate students. Because mathematics uses a special language, and in many cases uses that language in a special way, teachers must recognize the need to teach students to read and think in this language if they are to understand mathematics and to develop their skills. Teachers of the content areas such as physics, biology, mathematics, history, geography, art, music, and even English, all need to be intimately familiar with the language structures specific to their disciplines. One of their most important tasks is to teach their students to use these structures in their thinking, reading and writing.

Recently, I was in a senior high school talking to students about books and reading. As always happens, I was accosted on my way out the door, surrounded by kids confessing that they couldn't read, that they were disheartened and didn't know where to turn. As I always do, I left my e-mail address and, as always happens, I returned home to more confessions from distressed students. The following is one of those letters.

Dear Mr. Bouchard,

Thank you for coming and presenting at my school. You are a unique writer and a very inspiring person. I really enjoyed your talk with us.

I am in grade 12. I fall under the category of those who don't like reading. I hate it when a teacher calls on me to read in front of the class, I feel as if everyone is going to mock me because I read slowly and get words mixed up easily. I have never approached any of my teachers really because I'm sure they would always say, well you can read an easier book! Well I think them doing that has caused me to never want to try the harder novels. I have probably only read two or three full novels and that is probably including ones that I skipped a chapter or at least a few pages. I have such a great imagination and would love to enjoy reading.

My dad used to read to me all of the time when I was younger and I wish he still did. I enjoy short stories and things like that but I get bored easily and need something to really grab my attention.

I know I am rambling on, but I would really like your help in guiding me down what has been a hard and frustrating road — reading well and enjoying it.

One last thing I would like to add. Recently I have thought of taking up writing after I finish high school. I love writing in English, when they don't give you a topic you could write about anything in your imagination. We used to write weekly journals in English last semester and I got eleven out of ten every time. I never asked why I got the bonus mark but I

guessed he liked my writing. So I thought maybe writing was a
course in life I could take, at least the first course! :)

   Thank you for your time and I hope to hear from you in
the near future.

   Sincerely, Crystal

There is much that we as teachers can learn from this letter. We must avoid having students suffer the fear of being asked to read aloud in front of their peers, as this student did. We could ask for those who would enjoy having an opportunity to read aloud to volunteer or we could limit the audience by having children read aloud to groups of four or five. And, as I have mentioned earlier in this chapter, rather than have students afraid to approach us about their reading, or afraid that we might be critical of what they are currently reading, we must show an interest in learning about the kinds of books each of our students enjoys and seems equipped to handle.

Crystal tells us that she has a "great imagination," enjoys short stories and being read to, and "would really love to enjoy reading." What a gold mine of information throughout the letter for a teacher to build upon! Here is a student who really wants to become a reader and is open to suggestions that will lead to "reading well and enjoying it." As a parallel to encouraging students to read books that are of personal interest, many teachers have discovered that they get much stronger writing from their students when they allow them to choose the topics themselves.

In the next chapter, addressed to administrators, I will elaborate on some of the approaches that could be initiated by principals and teachers in both elementary and secondary schools to ensure that their students become readers and that their schools are recognized as being "reading schools" — schools in which books and reading are school-wide priorities. Administrators must become involved in literacy and reading, an area that the majority have long neglected and looked upon as someone else's responsibility.

Administrators, Districts and Schools

~ chapter 4 ~

ADMINISTRATORS, DISTRICTS AND SCHOOLS

A man who wants to lead the orchestra must
turn his back on the crowd.
— JAMES COOK

Administrators, many of you are not going to like what I have
to say. I become more and more convinced with every talk
that I give in schools, that administrators are, by and large, poor
role models when it comes to promoting literacy. With the influence
that you have over the whole school community, every choice you
make has great power. If you choose not to read, not to prioritize
reading in your school or schools, not to read to, and with, your staff
and students, then you are misusing your power and your position.

A MESSAGE TO MINISTRIES AND DEPARTMENTS OF EDUCATION

Your job is to oversee the teaching of our most treasured resource —
our children. Literacy is, without question, the cornerstone of every
person's education. The most important role of the school system is to
produce literate graduates. And the most important role of a ministry
or department of education is to watch over and guide that process.

*No book is really
worth reading at
the age of ten that is
not equally (and
often far more)
worth reading at
the age of fifty and
beyond.*

C.S. LEWIS

If you, the Ministry of Education, were doing your job effectively, you would openly discuss, plan for and make literacy a priority. You would place literacy at the forefront of everything you do. From the money that you allocate to individual school boards, to the resources that you make available, to the curriculum and the forms you require teachers to use as report cards, each and every one of these things should reflect your top priority — the promotion of literacy.

Instead, I see ministries and departments sidetracked by new initiatives such as programs to foster self-esteem, courses in career planning and a whole range of proposals brought forward by small, special interest groups. Dollars are being taken straight from budgets allocated for books and spent instead on technology.

Yet nothing fosters self-esteem better than success in the core subjects — reading, writing and numeracy. Nothing helps young people prepare for careers better than success in these very basic skills. Technology is important. It can even help children strengthen their reading and writing skills. But it must not come at the expense of books. And bureaucracy can be streamlined, with power and dollars placed in the hands of those who are in the best position to put them to use. It is time that you, our elected leaders, do everything you can to enable your school boards to focus on literacy.

A MESSAGE TO SCHOOL BOARDS

Students are graduating functionally illiterate and you have the power to do something about it. You may believe that you are stymied by limited budgets and by ministry or department directives that do not recognize the importance of literacy. But no matter what the obstacles may be, you have the power and the authority to make literacy the first priority.

First, each of you could make books a part of your life. All of your employees could be encouraged to commit themselves to learning to love to read and to modeling reading in their communities. You could work with schools, community centers and businesses to make reading a living part of your community — for adults and youth alike. You have the power to make dramatic changes.

Can you imagine the impact a superintendent would have on a group of principals and assistant principals if he or she were to start the year off by presenting each one of them with a copy of a popular children's book? A discussion of their reactions to the book would follow naturally, as would their distribution of that or another favorite to the teachers in their school. In such a way, a whole school district could read together.

Books are the main source of our knowledge, our reservoir of faith, memory, wisdom, morality, poetry, philosophy, history and science.

Daniel J. Boorstin

Is the word "literacy" in your mission statement? If it is not, it should be. Are teacher librarians valued in your district? Do they have enough time and money to do their jobs effectively? Are your secondary schools encouraged to prioritize literacy right through grade twelve? Do their budgets encourage them to buy new literature for teens? Are they actively exploring such books with their students or destroying their students' enthusiasm for reading with endless comprehension tests and book reports? Do you encourage all the schools in your district to bring in authors and illustrators and storytellers regularly?

You, even more than the ministry, the province, state or nationwide bodies responsible for education, are in an ideal position to influence your community. As district administrators, you can provide guidance for your schools. You can ensure that literacy is a top priority in every classroom, in every school and in your community as a whole.

THE ROLE OF SCHOOL-BASED ADMINISTRATORS

I would like to take a little more space to talk about what school-based administrators can do as I spent a large part of my career as a school principal and it was during those years that I believe I had

~ි~

*Children who are
not told stories and
who are not read to
will have few
reasons for wanting
to learn to read.*

GAIL HALEY

the greatest impact. School-based administrators have a far-reaching influence upon their students and the programs that govern their education. Along with that power comes responsibility. They are, each and every one, responsible for the literacy of their students. They hire. They direct programs and courses. They have influence by the very nature of their contacts and positions. If many of their children are weak readers, administrators must take responsibility for the situation and seek solutions to change it. Whether you are a parent, a teacher, or an administrator, look at the school system in your area and ask yourself if programs necessary to promote literacy and a love of reading are in place. Are the administrators in your area being guided by what I sometimes refer to as the three "Ms? Are they Modeling reading for their staff and students, taking steps to Motivate those they work with, and accepting responsibility for Managing their schools and districts? Spending time, money and energy on books and programs will not strengthen the literacy of young people if administrators have not created a literacy- and literature-rich environment or are not prepared to take leadership.

The principal's office

It is not merely difficult for administrators to hide their priorities and personalities; it is impossible. Just as our homes reflect who we are, so do our workplaces. Had you come into my office when I started working as a principal, you would have seen the real me. My office was filled with life, just as my classroom had been: hats hung from the ceiling, hats reflecting people and events. Dolls, bears and statues were displayed everywhere. Countless pictures of my children, my pets, and my family's hobbies and interests adorned the walls. Music poured forth from a cheap tape recorder. It was not the most professional of appearances, but it reflected who I was and what I was trying to say: "Welcome kids! This place is for you!"

Not long after I became an administrator, my office changed to reflect what I believed about my new role. Oh, a few remnants of the old me remained: pictures, posters, a few necessary hats, that kind of thing. But my bookshelves held every professional binder available to a principal. Like my colleagues, I had binders filled with reports, policy manuals, curriculum guides, handbooks on this and others on that; it might have appeared to be an administrator's heaven. But it was not. My office did not contain a single children's book. My heart was not yet where it should have been, nor was the focus of our school.

Show me the books he loves and I shall know the man far better than through mortal friends.

DAWN ADAMS

Parents, check out your school and district administrators' offices to see what I mean. Drop by the board office and ask to see your superintendent's office. Who are these people? What are their interests and what are their priorities? Your principal's office probably reveals little about him or her as a person. If the principal's office is without a single children's book, you might want to ask why. You might even begin to suspect that literacy is not a priority in this particular school.

Principals and vice-principals have significant power within our schools. In fact, they have a greater influence on the direction of a school than anyone else. Therefore, administrators are the people who must take a leadership role in promoting literacy and a love of literature in their schools.

A visitor to my office in the last five years of my principalship would have left saying, "Does he ever love children's books!" My office contained only my desk (phone and computer of course) and my books — my wall-to-wall, floor-to-ceiling collection of children's books. At one point we had a school contest to guess how many books were in my office. Our count revealed that I had more than twenty-three hundred books, ranging from picture books, fantasy and adventure to quality nonfiction. Every one of these books was available to anyone who cared to borrow it.

I viewed my collection and my reading aloud as catalysts for exciting children about literature. Additional titles by many of the authors, illustrators and poets in my collection were also available in the school and classroom libraries enabling children to extend the listening and reading experiences they had found especially rewarding. The key is to immerse children in books. Researchers have established that the more immediate the access to books, the greater the amount of recreational reading done by children. In three similar studies in the 1980s, referred to as the "Book Flood" studies, classrooms were "flooded" with quality trade books, as opposed to assigned reading and textbooks, and teachers were asked to encourage free selection and reading by their students. Each of the studies reported improvement in children's reading achievement, gains in comprehension and vocabulary, increased voluntary reading, and better attitudes toward reading than exhibited by children in comparison schools that did not participate in the research.

From the hallway of our school, visitors often mistook my office for the library. My message was clear to all including our students: books are a priority in my life and in our school. Our students knew, their parents knew and so did our teachers. Our vice-principal kindly agreed to house all my administrative binders and guides in her office along with her own personal collection of children's books.

Reading to children

While books and reading became my focus over time, they are not the focus of most administrators. Principals or superintendents who read aloud to children are rare. So are educational administrators who keep up with the best and most popular children's books of the day. How many have read J.K. Rowling's Harry Potter books or the Redwall series by Brian Jacques, for example? Life is fast and complicated in the school principal's office, just as it is in the offices of district staff. Few administrators find time to do what they must, model good reading practices. Like others involved in promoting literacy, school administrators must begin to read for pleasure and they must be seen doing it. They must put aside some of those important tasks on their desks and read. And because they work with youth, they must read, among other things, that which has been written for young people.

Unfortunately, I have met few administrators who read children's books. They read educational journals, newly-developed curricular materials sent out by higher-level officials, and promotional materials from educational and commercial suppliers. Leaders whose purpose it is to enrich the lives of young people do not take the time or appear to have the desire to get into the reading world of those for whom they are responsible.

Administrators can read children's books and model reading for their students if they choose to do so. From the superintendent through to the school-based administrator, they can establish their own priorities. The truth is that they tend to view reading as a pleasurable pastime rather than as a valuable educational activity and, therefore, not as something that should take place during working hours. It would be difficult for most administrative officers to picture themselves reading children's stories, let alone having someone else see them doing it!

I am now convinced that the best thing children could see me, as a principal, doing is reading children's books, both to myself and to them. Years ago I converted a tin cookie box into a treasure chest. It was large enough to hold twenty to thirty children's books, yet small enough to carry around. In it I gathered some of my favorite books and it sat prominently in my office ready to be called on when needed.

That box was needed every day! As school principal, I had the freedom to share favorite books with whomever I chose. Of course, I chose all the children in the school. I scheduled regular blocks of time for reading to children. Twenty percent of my day, every day,

There is creative reading as well as creative writing.

RALPH WALDO EMERSON

was spent doing the most important and the most enjoyable part of my job — reading to kids. I was forever seeking out new, exciting books to share with children.

I would pick up my book box and hit the hallways. When classes saw me come around the corner with my treasure chest under my arm, they would applaud. The teacher would take a planned break and I would do what I had grown to love to do best; I would read to wide-eyed, appreciative children.

How I would have loved to have been a superintendent, just for a few days, to find my way into various schools with my favorite books. I can only begin to imagine the impact that I could have had with kids, teachers, parents and school-based administrators. Talk about modeling! Upon seeing the response of the children, teachers and principals could not help but follow my example. I am sad to say, however, that superintendents who model reading aloud in the schools in their district are rare indeed. Yet the impact that I witnessed is within the reach of each and every one. It is truly an example of actions speaking more loudly than words. The time devoted to an activity is regarded as a measure of its worth. Think of the inherent message communicated to students when teachers and administrators give reading aloud to them priority in a school day.

I spend significant time speaking to groups of children. I talk about poetry and the richness of the English language. I speak about the appeal of pictures in books. I talk to kids of all ages about the thrills and joys of writing in the hopes of getting them reading and writing. Many schools can only afford a visit such as mine once a year or less. Yet, in the schools I visit, administrators almost never take or make the time to listen to me talk to their students.

By not attending my talks, administrators are sending a clear message to their staff and students — the message that reading is not important enough for them to take an interest or be involved.

And once I am gone, they are not in a position to engage in a single conversation with a teacher or with a child about the substance of what I said.

It will be a day to celebrate when I can speak to administrators and get past the first stage, which is encouraging them to feel responsible for promoting literacy and literature. The second stage will involve sharing ideas and methods for promoting literacy — successes that are working for our colleagues across the continent. The third stage will be wonderful. I imagine the day when I will be invited to speak to administrators about my books. Administrators could benefit greatly from talking with children's writers about how we write what we write and from exchanging with us ideas and the passion for books. The day those things begin to happen will be a day to celebrate. On that day our kids will set out on the road to becoming lifelong readers.

Promoting literature and reading

Administrators must remember that their attitude and focus are key to the attitude and focus of their schools. For schools to become places where literacy and literature are valued, administrators must motivate teachers and students alike to assess and, where necessary, change their priorities. Teachers, parents and students are influenced by school-based administrators. Parents, for example, benefit from communication with their children's schools. They are willing to listen, willing to consider, if principals give them something to listen to. Principals can communicate with parents through voice mail, through the Internet, through newsletters and a centrally located bulletin board in the school dedicated to messages to parents.

Administrators have the power to make literacy their schools' focus simply by bringing up the subject. So I say to them, bring it up! Talk about it at every turn. Make reading fun. Make it exciting.

*But words are
things, and a small
drop of ink,*

*Falling like dew,
upon a thought,
produces*

*That which makes
thousands, perhaps
millions, think.*

LORD BYRON

Make it your priority. Speak to parents about modeling and reading with children in their homes. Talk to teachers and parents about literacy-related programs and opportunities. Review books, discuss authors, promote your local bookstores and libraries, and publish lists of favorite books. Most school districts today have students from homes in which languages other than English are spoken; it is crucial that any information related to the school, such as the suggestions above, be accessible to all parents. Administrators must ensure that, through the assistance of translators, school bulletins and newsletters, open house and teacher-parent sessions, parent advisory committee meetings, and day-to-day contacts can be understood by all the parents whose children attend the school.

Everyone loves lists. We all find our attention caught by lists such as these: the ten best and the ten worst dressed at the Oscars; the most respected and the least respected Canadian prime ministers or American presidents; David Letterman's top tens; A & E's best cities; the healthiest foods; the best restaurants. Why not circulate lists of favorite books in our schools? You might consider a list of the favorite books of the week, of each student in the senior class or of each child in grade three. The custodian's favorite children's book of the week, the secretary's, the lunchtime supervisor's and the volleyball coach's could be shared regularly.

Lists are catchy and easy to create. Annotated lists of Wendy's and my favorite books to read aloud to children are available at the end of this book. When I was a principal, I made a list of my favorites available to our school community through our weekly bulletin. To reach the broader community, our local bookstore owner agreed to post the list next to her front counter. Lists of students' and staffs' favorites could also be circulated. Parents and students are interested in and informed by the recommendations and tastes of others.

The administrator's focus on reading must be front and center in the school. The school's budget should reflect a focus on reading.

Schools are not only being asked to cut expenses, they are often asked to absorb the cost of various technologies. If books and programs that focus on literacy are not held sacrosanct, they will be eroded. In fact such erosion is happening everywhere. Technology is important of course, but not at the expense of books. And the principal is the one with the power to maintain a balance. He or she is in the position to authorize book purchases, author visits and necessary fundraisers. The principal must not only be supportive; he or she must take a position of leadership. Without the support of school-based administrators, teacher librarians will find it difficult to hold on to the little funding that they have left, let alone to lobby for more. In fact, lobbying for school library funding is the responsibility of the entire school community, not just the librarian. Teachers, students and parents must work together to ensure that the school's library resources are both maintained and kept current.

Although the major leadership and responsibility for direction and priorities in the school rest with the principal, he or she has a wealth of human resources — teachers, students and support staff — to depend upon for help in identifying and implementing school-wide initiatives such as those related to books and reading. An open-library policy that permits students to go to the library throughout the day rather than at set times has proven to be rewarding in many schools. For reading to be an integral part of each school day, books must not only be available but easily accessible. Attractive, interest-catching book displays and book talks in the library and individual classrooms are just two of the ways in which teacher librarians generate enthusiasm for voluntary reading. In a newsletter to parents, the library's goals were outlined as follows:

1. To make the library a comfortable place for the
   children to learn.

2. To make the library a natural extension of the classroom program.

3. To provide library resources to support the curriculum.

4. To help students develop research and study skills.

5. To encourage the love of books and reading for pleasure.

Time and time again when the librarian selects a collection of books to introduce to a class, the interest is so immediate that he or she leaves the classroom empty-handed. We are all interested in learning about books that others have found interesting. For example, as early as grade one, children browse the return book bin to see what schoolmates have been reading.

Many teachers provide class time for children to share books they have particularly enjoyed and would recommend, with posted lists of favorites becoming a natural extension of this activity. Loose-leaf binders of book covers and brief comments written by both teachers and students are also popular resources for students looking for a book to read. Often teachers collaborate and have students from different classes visit to introduce their current favorites through mini book talks. "Buddy-reading" programs, in which students from one class are paired with children in another, for example grade six students with grade two youngsters, have also proven to be highly successful for all involved. Beginning each day with a short literary excerpt chosen and read alternately by teachers and students in the classroom or school assembly, is another effective way of generating an interest in reading. Just be sure that the books being introduced are available for borrowing, either from the library or the reader.

School-based administrators are not the only ones who have the power to motivate. District administrators should involve themselves, not only by being seen as readers and by reading to children, but also by considering and supporting at the district level many of my suggestions to principals. Why not spend district professional development dollars on bringing in children's authors and illustrators to speak to groups of teachers? Invite publishers' representatives to showcase their books for young people. If a district's mission statement doesn't mention the words "literacy," "literature" or "book," I maintain that it should. School and district administrators began their careers as teachers. As they assume their new roles and responsibilities, they must not abandon the priorities that informed and influenced their teaching. Literacy is indisputably the cornerstone of learning; administrators must never lose sight of its primacy when initiating and implementing school and district initiatives.

A number of years ago, Wendy took part in a successful district-wide initiative to promote reading in the small city of Prince Rupert in northern British Columbia. Schools and community groups worked together to stage the "Pull the Plug" campaign in which families pledged to turn the television set off for an entire week. People picked up their pledge cards, their bookmarks and a button — a TV set within a circle with a diagonal line through it — at their work place or the public library. A huge "Pull the Plug" banner spanned the main street, sweatshirts with the logo were evident everywhere in town, and a pamphlet titled "Handbook for Survival: What To Do When the Screen Goes Blank ..." complete with a "Help Hot Line," was provided to all participants. The District Reading and Writing Network Committee organizing the event made it clear that it was not attacking television but regarded the "Pull the Plug" week as an opportunity for parents and children to engage in some of the leisure time activities enjoyed before television dominated family life. During the week, which immediately preceded Prince Rupert's nine-day Book Festival Celebration, each school had creative displays and events focusing on

books and reading for pleasure. As the support and enthusiasm for books and reading continued to be apparent in homes, schools, businesses and the public library following these special events, the district-wide initiative was acknowledged to have been a great success.

While programs such as the above are impressive, administrators are faced with dozens of issues and priorities — many very specific to the schools and communities in which they operate. Not all principals can or will choose to put literacy at the top of their list. Still, even if literacy is not at the forefront, it should occupy at least some time in their day and space in their offices. A few token shelves in the principal's office highlighting favorite children's books or a ten minute session each week reading aloud to the kindergarten class would be a start.

A contributor to the International Reading Association's bi-monthly newsletter, *Reading Today*, Anthony D. Fredericks argues that by stepping into the role of model, the principal can have

The Rise and Fall of a "Word Wall"

WENDY: In addition to the many activities involving the Prince Rupert community during "Pull the Plug" week and the nine-day Book Festival Celebration, each school had its own special reading and language projects. At Pineridge, one of the elementary schools I enjoyed visiting, the principal, David Vick, initiated a unique language project for the older girls and boys. They were challenged to build on the school playground a "word wall" with pieces of two-by-four, a wall that, when completed, would be put to a test of strength by a large, flatbed truck. On each piece of wood the students wrote their favorite words from their writing dictionaries or their reading. They were wonderfully enthusiastic, spurred by the oddly tangible juxtaposition of language, blocks of wood and a great big truck. Needless to say, the entire school and many parents were present to enjoy the spectacle. The wall did not survive. The words did.

Their favorite words
make a wall.

The wall stands ready.

The wall is down.
The words remain.

photos by Wendy Sutton

greater, more far-reaching influence than is to be had by issuing directives or taking other more authoritative approaches. If a principal demonstrates a genuine passion for reading and for good books, he or she will be in a strong position to help initiate and work together with the staff and parents to implement programs designed to promote literacy and to create lifelong readers.

Implementing recreational silent reading

Many different programs and strategies are used in schools guided by people who care about literacy, but one that is often found in such schools, one that I believe no school should be without, is a school-based, silent-reading program. Acronyms vary, but include USSR (Uninterrupted Sustained Silent Reading), FVR (Free Voluntary Reading), DEAR (Drop Everything And Read), DIRT (Daily Individual Reading Time) and SQUIRT (Sustained Quiet Uninterrupted Reading Time). A successful secondary school program with the acronym START (Students and Teachers All Reading Together) highlights the involvement of the teachers in the program. Other specifics may vary as well. In most cases silent reading takes place every day for fifteen to twenty minutes. Many schools have silent reading after lunch, but others have chosen different times, depending on the rhythm of their day.

What must not vary, however, is the universality of the program. Everyone in the school must read at the same time, including the administrators. Among its many benefits, such a program pulls everyone in the school community together, giving them a shared interest and objective — to help young people become enthusiastic, voluntary, lifelong readers. Teaching children to read becomes almost pointless if we do not instill in them a desire to read. Unfortunately, too many school districts gauge children's reading achievement with standardized reading tests rather than giving consideration to the personal reading habits of their students. Too frequently children are taught to read but are not encouraged to develop the love and habit of reading. Consequently, they often leave school functionally illiterate.

In *The Power of Reading*, Stephen Krashen suggests that illiteracy can be cured by one simple activity — free voluntary reading: "When children and less literate adults read for pleasure, even fifteen minutes a day in school, their reading comprehension, writing style, vocabulary, speaking and control of grammar improve and they find academic texts easier to use." Citing numerous and varied studies, Krashen demonstrates that a voluntary reading program is a more powerful means of developing readers than direct instruction with drills and exercises.

No matter how busy you may think you are, you must find time for reading, or surrender yourself to self-chosen ignorance.

ATWOOD H. TOWNSEND

In schools where recreational reading is nurtured, conversations such as the following become regular occurrences:

"'Oh, hi, Mr. Bouchard. I'm reading Avi's new book about Poppy. Have you read it?'

'No, I haven't. Tell me about it.'

'Well, Poppy is a little mouse. She has all kinds of adventures in the first books. She even wins out against an owl. My favorite part of this new one ...'"

Such conversations are just waiting to happen!

As an administrator, a teacher, a parent and one interested in turning all children on to reading, I feel strongly that every school, elementary and secondary, must have a silent-reading program. I spoke earlier of the difficulties, such as controlling television viewing, that many parents have when trying to create an atmosphere at home in which children can enjoy a good, quiet read. If children experience the pleasures of reading to themselves in a conducive environment at school, they will be more likely to support the creation of the same environment at home.

On the other hand, many studies have found that a stimulating literacy environment at home contributes to children's voluntary interest in reading and literature. A body of research focused on children who began school with an early interest in books and were already able to read without having received direct instruction. The studies found that these children came from homes rich with books and had parents who were readers and read to them regularly. Research has also found that children in schools that promoted voluntary reading did more reading at home than did children from schools in which there was little emphasis on silent, recreational reading.

Many researchers have established that there is a positive correlation between voluntary, leisure reading and reading achievement and that teachers play a critical role in shaping children's attitudes toward reading. Over twenty years ago an extensive UNESCO study, *Promoting Voluntary Reading for Children and Young People,* concluded: "The role of teachers in stimulating voluntary reading among children and young people is … potentially the most powerful of all adult influences upon the young." In addition to the value of teachers' modeling positive reading behaviors, research has also identified the practice of reading to children daily and actively engaging them with literature as being fundamental to developing enthusiastic, voluntary readers.

Sadly many schools today do not offer silent-reading programs. Common excuses lie in the heavy demands of the curriculum and the ever-increasing non-instructional responsibilities being passed along to teachers. Administrators should consider it their role to help teachers cope with these demands and to communicate to the school community the educational value of devoting twenty minutes a day to silent, recreational reading.

Of everything we do in our schools, few programs are as pleasing to witness as an uninterrupted silent-reading program! Parents and other visitors to our school commented continually on the warm, quiet, productive atmosphere evident during our silent-reading period. The key elements are as follows:

1. Students and adults alike read in total quiet. The program should run for between fifteen and twenty minutes at the same time daily. Classroom doors are left open and students are asked to clear their desks of all materials but those they have brought to read. Secondary schools with USSR programs have found that having the silent-reading block take place at the beginning of a class is most effective; when it takes place at the end of a class, the time frequently is eroded by last minute instructions and students packing up their materials. Having silent reading at the beginning of class also allows time for a brief sharing of titles or comments with teachers and fellow students. In secondary schools because of their size, a PA announcement usually signals the beginning of the silent-reading period.

2. Students and adults are free to select their own books, magazines or newspaper articles but must have their materials with them when the actual reading period begins. Although students can bring whatever they choose, once a comfortable reading atmosphere has been established, the benefits of the program are enhanced when teachers encourage students to extend their reading options by introducing a range of genres for them to consider — biographies, poetry, fiction and nonfiction. Some schools ask students to bring only books but allow a weekly "free day" when they can bring magazines and newspapers.

3. Crucial to the success of the program is that EVERYONE in the school participates: students, teachers, secretaries, school engineers,

administrators, teaching assistants and visitors in the school. Signs are posted at entrances to the school notifying visitors of the need for complete silence during the time period stated. Deliveries can be left at the door and school board workers can be asked to take their coffee break away from the school. Ideally the school should be completely quiet.

4. These silent-reading sessions are not evaluated or reported on. However, by showing an interest and keeping informal notes, teachers have an ideal opportunity to learn more about their students and their reading preferences — information that can help them extend students' reading experiences by recommending titles and authors. Brief, informal discussions of favorite books, and of literary and critical issues related to the reading of older students, have been found to heighten an interest in books and voluntary reading. Students also can be encouraged to keep a record of books and authors they have particularly enjoyed. However, whatever variations are introduced, if the objectives of the program are to be realized, it is essential that the time devoted daily to silent, recreational reading be pleasurable for all involved.

If your school has failed, in its wisdom and planning, to find a few minutes every day to change gears and allow children time to read, it must shift priorities. Many teachers try to make up for the lack of a school-wide program by offering silent-reading programs within their classrooms. And so they should, but they should not have to. The school needs to set priorities so that all children enjoy the benefits of such a program — one that is never displaced by

Show an Interest in What Young People Read

WENDY: I have always been interested in the reading interests and preferences of young people. Consequently, when our student teachers were on their teaching practica, I had the opportunity to visit many elementary and secondary classrooms and to observe first hand what students were choosing to read. Once, during USSR in a secondary classroom, I asked the teacher's permission to walk around the room to make a list of the books the students had chosen to read. She admitted that she was surprised and embarrassed that a total stranger was showing more interest in what her students were reading than she ever had but then offered to help me collect titles. Even during that one session, she engaged three of her students in brief conversations about the books they were reading and appeared to be looking forward to talking with others in the class about their books and what they liked to read.

other school-wide activities. The principal is responsible for initiating, supporting and protecting the silent-reading program.

Getting such a program started is not necessarily easy. For a school-wide, silent-reading program to be successful, the teaching staff must be fully committed to supporting it. Many study and question-answer sessions, workshops, and presentations by teachers from schools that have such programs may need to take place before an administrator will achieve the necessary commitment from his or her staff to be able to initiate such a program. Teachers have to be convinced that devoting a block of time daily to silent reading by both the students and themselves is a worthwhile use of teaching time. Once the majority of the teachers have opted to implement and support a school-wide, silent-reading program, all staff members are obligated to let students read silently during the designated time and, hopefully, to read themselves. Although you as the principal will also be modeling silent reading, during the first week or so of the introduction of the program, particularly in a secondary school, it may be necessary to ensure that students are not in the halls or stairwells but have settled quickly in their classrooms.

In my last few years as principal, I started the year off by notifying our parents of this very important program. Our school would slow its pace from 10:40 to 11:00 AM every day. Everything else would stop and everyone would read. Only one telephone line would be left open. We asked that parents only call in case of an emergency during these sacred minutes. If they had to pick up a child for an appointment, they were asked to arrange a time outside of our silent-reading program.

We made a point of getting our kindergarten students participating right away. In September, we toured our morning kindergartners around the school, showing them that everyone read silently at this time. They started out by reading for ten minutes and gradually worked up to twenty. Although we felt that having our USSR program take place in the morning emphasized its importance, we also wanted to involve our afternoon kindergarten children. They had their own silent-reading period every day, but once a month we held USSR in the afternoon and invited the afternoon Ks to come to the school library. The arrangement made the youngsters feel that they were special members of the school. Every day we wrapped up silent reading with a piece of classical music played throughout the school. Parent observers often commented on the humane and nurturing atmosphere the music created.

Involving teachers and parents

If, as an administrator, you are uncertain as to how to get started promoting literacy in your school, a silent-reading program is an excellent place to start. You might want to look at Gail Heald-Taylor's *Administrator's Guide to Whole Language* for some other ideas. At the same time, work on building your own collection of quality children's books and create opportunities to share those books with children in each class. You might want to look at the following titles as well as explore several of the books listed in the bibliography. Marie Clay's *An Observation Survey of Literacy Achievement* and *Literacy for a Diverse Society: Perspectives, Practices and Policies*, edited by E.H. Hiebert, are both excellent resources.

Once you have read a few professional references share key excerpts with your staff and parents. The books will provide you with both theory and practical advice and will help teachers and parents to understand and support your philosophy.

What follows is another excerpt from one of my school bulletins. Perhaps reading about my commitment will help you begin to develop your own philosophy.

We will either find a way, or make one.

HANNIBAL

The principal's role and responsibilities:

1. Children need to see the principal reading. They need to see and believe that reading is important to me and that it is a big part of my life. I must model good reading practices.

2. I must provide teachers with the resources necessary to implement a sound reading program. In some cases, our budget makes it difficult for us to acquire the books we need to promote reading in our school. We therefore appeal to our PAC members to support our school and classroom libraries. For two consecutive years they have helped us reach our goal.

3. I create programs and support existing ones that promote a sound reading environment: We have several exciting programs in place:
    • START (our silent-reading program),
    • Pajama party (our annual evening featuring local authors and illustrators),
    • The principal's guarantee that all intermediate children can name the book they are currently reading and its author. (Anyone is welcome to challenge this guarantee. Simply seek me out and together we will stop five children at random. If one fails to name the book and author he or she is reading at the time, I will give you one of my books. If the children succeed, you can give me a children's book for my collection. Children enjoy the challenge game and take a certain delight in seeing me have to give up a book when on the rare occasion one of them "fails.")

4. I share my Principal's Collection daily with children, staff and parents.

5. I read to children daily.

6. In the hallways, the gym, and the classroom or on the playground, I talk with children about books, authors and illustrators.

7. I publish lists of favorite books of some of our children, parents, and staff.

8. I work to ensure that everyone — teachers parents and children — stay committed to each of our literacy programs.

Many principals find themselves in schools and communities where resources are limited and parents have little left once they have fed and clothed their children. Getting books into homes that need them should be one of the school's priorities. Direct requests to students and parents for donations of books that they are willing to pass along to other readers can be surprisingly successful. Ensuring that needy children are encouraged to take books home to read to themselves or to family members is another approach. The sensitive pairing of reading buddies where one child has book resources to share with the other is also effective. For schools in which many of the children are from homes in which English is not the first language, foreign language collections of children's books are essential. Children who speak other languages should have the same opportunity as English-speaking children to

Scheduling Can Be Flexible and Creative

WENDY: When I was teaching in an elementary school in West Vancouver, I was lucky enough to have colleagues and a principal who were willing to consider alternate ways of structuring our classes and time. We had four classes of combined grades six and seven and were particularly aware of the strain on the library resources when all four classes needed access to the same materials — we only had so many books on Egypt! Dubbing our plan the "Sutton Semester System" (SSS), we decided that two of the classes would take language arts and social studies the first term while the other two took science and math, and that the classes would switch subjects and teachers for the second term. Another advantage of this arrangement was the flexibility possible within any day or week. For example, if our students were deeply involved in what they were doing, my social studies partner or I would ask to keep the class for the entire morning rather than switching after recess. And, as we were working with the same children, many of the major projects evolved as a combination of our two subject areas. Happily, the arrangement worked well for math and science as well. At the end of the year, we all found that focusing on only two major subjects at a time made teaching and learning more personally rewarding.

read for pleasure in their own language.

Much of the direction in every child's education comes from his or her teachers, who, in turn, get much of their direction from their administrators. It is the role and responsibility of administrators to initiate and maintain communication with parents. Likewise, it is our role to offer guidance and support for approaches we know are essential to their children's learning to read. Objectives that promote literacy in the school and in the community must be clearly articulated early in the school year. And the leadership for these initiatives must come from administrators.

Building on personal strengths

One of the most positive experiences that I had during my career as a principal is directly related to reading and writing and is testimony to the deepest meaning of "teaching to a child's strengths." While every school principal will not find the following activity suited to him or her, every school principal can develop a program to promote literacy school-wide, to complement what teachers are doing in their classrooms and to provide much needed support.

I used one of my books, *A Barnyard Bestiary*, a picture book that combines poetry and fine art, to model the writing, illustrating and publishing process for my students and to motivate them to produce their own books. *Bestiary* had not yet been released, so the children got an early peak at it.

The first step was to ask that every division in our school select a "gifted artist" and a "gifted writer" to participate in a publishing experience. This creative child would ideally be one who was not the all-round, academic, straight A student. I requested that teachers select children who were known to their classmates as the "artists," not necessarily the "academics." These kids exist in every class. You simply have to ask the class who the artists are. They'll turn and point to them. And ninety-five percent of the time, it is a child who is not the athlete or the academic, just the artist. I relied on the teachers to be selective and it did work out that the students who came to me were, with the exception of two, just artists. Creative children tend to receive little positive recognition at school for their God-given gifts. Like so many others, they too often have to wait until they leave school to find comfort and success in their special abilities.

For twelve weeks, I started Monday off by calling for our gifted artists, authors and poets to come down to my office. I was intentional in using the word "gifted." It meant a great deal to each child selected to hear himself or herself called "gifted" and to have the rest of the class hear it too.

There is an important lesson here. Every child should have his or her gifts and skills applauded daily. We — parents, teachers, administrators, all of us — must discover the gifts in every child and mirror those gifts back to that child at every opportunity. I was told that one little girl in grade two stood before her classmates, walked clear across the room away from the door and then turned, walked back to the door and left. She made sure that everyone saw her, the gifted girl. Unfortunately, that little girl's experience of having her special talents recognized is not usual. The children who receive daily pats on the back in our schools continue to be those who can read and write and, therefore, are able to succeed at the particular tasks we place before them.

Once I had gathered the writers and artists, we worked together to write, illustrate and self-publish a series of poems in a book similar in form to the book that I had just written. I took them through the same process that I had been through. We talked about media and resources. We shared ideas. Then we did our own thing. They created two books, both entitled *Barnyard Beauties*, published by Pauline Johnson Elementary. We had them professionally printed and bound — enough copies so that anyone interested might buy one. We sold them for fifteen dollars each. The

Bringing children and poetry together can be one of the most exciting experiences in parenting or teaching. Over the years, however, I have noted in too many cases what I have coined the DAM approach – Dissecting, Analyzing, and meaninglessly Memorizing poetry to death.

LEE BENNETT HOPKINS, *PASS THE POETRY, PLEASE*

project cost our school less than three hundred dollars. And I would do it again had it cost three thousand.

Not every principal has a children's book coming out that can be used as a model for a rich reading and writing activity. But every principal does have gifts and resources to draw upon. Every principal can share himself or herself with the students who are most in need. Every principal can walk down the hall with a favorite book, or a whole box of them, under his arm. And go outside and be seen reading at recess. And pop into the kindergarten class, or the grade seven class, to share a brand new picture book. And call the staff together to discuss what they would like to do school-wide and how they could most effectively reach out to parents. Every principal can and I believe should make literacy the top priority in his or her school.

Qualities of a "reading school"

At the end of Chapter 3 I refer to "reading schools," schools in which books and reading are clearly evident as being school-wide priorities. While at UBC, Wendy asked her student teachers to write a brief profile of the schools in which they did their practice teaching by answering the question, "What evidence was there that reading is important or encouraged in your school?" The descriptions of their experiences in both elementary and secondary schools are most revealing and informative and I think convincingly support the underlying premise and goal of this book. The following are excerpts from some of those school profiles.

★ Yes, my school is a reading school. Staff and students participate in a USSR program (the teachers read too). The librarian works cooperatively with teachers to help provide appropriate books for students. The library is always open. Teachers read a wide variety of books aloud daily. The librarian works with classes and small groups to make them aware of new books and displays.

★ My secondary school has implemented a school-wide silent-reading program. Each day I looked forward to twenty minutes of pleasurable reading. If only more of the grade eight students I observed shared my enthusiasm!

All that mankind has done, thought, gained or been; it is lying as in magic preservation in the pages of books.

THOMAS CARLYLE

The two English classrooms where I spent time had a positive atmosphere that encouraged students to read. Both contained book carousels filled with books that the classroom teachers had personally chosen. One of the teachers always placed new and interesting books of fiction and nonfiction on the blackboard shelf and would encourage students to look at and borrow them. Both teachers took time from their own reading to walk around the classroom, taking a look at what students were bringing to read, asking them about the books, what they particularly liked about them, and discussing them a bit if they had read them. Both teachers enthusiastically promoted reading as a fun activity.

★ At a community secondary school, many factors identified it as a reading school: a silent-reading period every day; an excellent, knowledgeable and enthusiastic librarian; a well-stocked school library (with many Canadian titles); and a public library attached to the school. I was encouraged by the informal chats I had with students about Canadian authors and books. The students are interested and willing but need to be encouraged.

★ Although my secondary school does not have a silent-reading program, I found it had a positive climate for reading. The library is well laid out and roomy. It is usually busy and the atmosphere is friendly and comfortable. I enjoyed talking with students about their reading. One grade nine boy's face lit up while he told me about the book he had just finished and asked me if I knew of others like it. A grade ten girl admitted that she didn't like to read until she read Mary Razzell's *Snow Apples*. Now she loves to read romantic stories and is always asking the librarian for suggestions ... My sponsor teacher reads aloud to his class and I read aloud to them as well.

★ I was in an immersion school where the teachers used to insist students read in French during USSR. However, having to read in French made them dread silent reading, rather than fostering a love of French literature. Therefore, teachers decided to allow students to read in the language of their choice; not surprisingly, several chose English novels. I read young adult fiction during silent reading; the students were interested in what I was reading and often wanted to read it after I was finished ... One thing I observed that does *not* work is silent reading without the teacher's participation. Lack of a good role model does not promote good habits.

★ My school is an academically oriented secondary school that is proud of its high graduation rate and its record of awards. Everywhere I saw students reading (or cramming for exams). The library is certainly well used. At all hours of the day it is full of students with books in front of them, enjoying the reading-oriented atmosphere and wealth of information to be found there. Some of my students would arrive at class with open books in their hands!

On the other hand, the absence of a structured silent-reading program took away from the impression that reading was a valued activity at the school. Reading seemed to be as regarded as something that just happened without any official encouragement. In this age of television, video and computers, we all need to be encouraged to read for knowledge AND entertainment.

★ Although my school allots twenty minutes of each English class to USSR, the teachers I observed did not participate. They used the time to mark or take attendance. My sponsor teacher, who claimed to be an avid reader, had no novels available that were not on the curriculum. The classroom bookshelves held old textbooks (rarely if ever used), Coles Notes for Shakespeare, and extra copies of the text currently being read.

The teacher librarian lived by a different philosophy. He encouraged students to spend time in the library for any reason, be it to read for pleasure, do research, finish homework, socialize, or discuss a personal problem. He kept his desk in an open area of the library, not behind the checkout counter. His unintimidating, friendly manner encouraged students to ask for assistance.

These varied descriptions reveal that the characteristics of reading schools are evident in our secondary schools. At the same time, many lack a silent-reading program, and many classrooms, even

English classrooms, contain no good books for the students to read — no evidence that the teacher him- or herself is a reader. What is happening in the classrooms and the library in your school, or the schools in your district or your province or your state? Ask yourself the same question that these student teachers took with them into their practicum: "Is your school a reading school?"

Whether you are a parent, a teacher or an administrator, an aunt, a grandfather, a school engineer, a neighbor or a friend, now that you have finished reading this book, the time to take action has arrived. If you are not now a lover of books and reading, you can and must become one. Whatever you choose to read, turn off the TV, ignore the phone, curl up in a chair or stretch out on the lawn and read. Then, make a date with yourself at the local library or children's bookstore and start looking for the children's books that both you and the young people in your life will love. The librarian and bookstore proprietor are waiting to assist you.

Once you have one children's book that you love in your hands, your next task is to bring the children within your influence together with books in an enduring relationship. You may be in a position to reach out to one child, or to thousands. Whichever the case, you have an important role to play.

Happy reading!

A Selection of David's Favorite Books for Reading Aloud

(in order of preference)

Picture Books

Knots on a Counting Rope by Bill Martin, Jr. and John Archambault.
(Gr.1-7)
This is the perfect read aloud for a beginning teacher or parent or
for anyone who is just getting started to reading aloud. I know of
several teachers who, after reading the book to their class, began
tying knots in their own counting ropes every time they read a
new story. The tears that it will bring to your eye are a bonus.

The Hockey Sweater by Roch Carrier. Illustrated by Sheldon Cohen.
A Canadian classic. Illustrated by one of Canada's best ever.

Pies by Wilma Riley. Illustrated by Sheldon Cohen. (Gr.2-7)
Started out as a wonderful short film by Canada's National Film
Board. The author, Wilma Riley, is a delight both as a writer
and as an individual. The book addresses cultural diversity and
appeals both in its honesty and in use of language. There isn't a
grade four boy anywhere who won't enjoy this read.

The Cat in the Hat by Dr. Seuss.
No other author has ever quite mastered the rhythm and
playfulness of Dr. Seuss' writing.

White Dynamite and Curly Kid by Bill Martin, Jr. and John
Archambault. Illustrated by Ted Rand. (Gr.1-7)
Like *The Paper Bag Princess*, this is a book that all children
should read. Bill Martin, Jr.'s language is simply marvelous.

Dreams Are More Real Than Bathtubs by Susan Musgrave.
Illustrated by Marie-Louise Gay. (K-3)
The language has the appeal of Barbara Park's *Skinnybones*. The
images are what this fine artist loves to create; they are "off the
wall." Bonus: they are both Canadians!

A Child's Treasury of Nursery Rhymes, illustrated by Kady
Macdonald Denton. (Conception-Gr.2)
Every wee one needs a collection of nursery rhymes. Every
Canadian home with wee ones should have this Governor
General's Award winner on their shelves.

Barnyard Dance by Sandra Boynton.
I so enjoy reading her books aloud to the very young. At this
point in our three-year-old's life, Boynton is her favorite (and
that makes her mine as well).

The Ghost-Eye Tree by Bill Martin, Jr. and John Archambault.
Illustrated by Ted Rand.
I heard Bill Martin, Jr. tell this one at a conference of whole
language teachers ten years ago. It remains one of my favorites
to this day. Try it … you can't help but love it.

Brown Bear, Brown Bear by Bill Martin, Jr. Illustrated by Eric Carle.
Bill Martin Jr. has given so much to children's literature. This
book is a classic. Martin's use of language is masterful. Eric
Carle is one of the best.

NOVELS

Harry Potter and the Philosopher's Stone and the series by J.K.
Rowling. (Gr.3-Adult)
My favorite book of all time! Never before has a single series of
books done so much to get kids reading. Everyone, everywhere
who is involved with children must read these books.

Harris and Me by Gary Paulsen. (Gr.6-9)
The best single read aloud you will ever find. Paulsen's language and perspective are a little risqué, so be prepared.

Skinnybones by Barbara Park. (Gr.2-8)

Another awesome read aloud. When you've scored big on this one, follow it up with ***Almost Starring Skinnybones***. What a talented writer!

The Twits (and ***Dirty Beasts*** and ***Matilda***) by Roald Dahl. (Gr.3-8)
The Twits is another book that is sure to offend some, and somewhat like the Goosebumps books, it really doesn't matter! Dahl's books offer some color to those who find many books beige.

The Hobbit by J.R.R. Tolkien. (Gr.4-Adult)
The Hobbit is right up there next to Harry Potter for kid appeal! (Also available on a wonderful audiotape in the BBC's "The Mind's Eye" series. And yes, "The Mind's Eye" has also done *The Lord of the Rings*!)

Charlotte's Web by E.B. White. (Gr.1-7)
This is another classic and truly one of my favorite read alouds. If you've not read *Charlotte's Web*, blush and then go fetch it. (A version is also available on tape read by E.B. White. To hear most authors read their work is a pleasure. To hear this man read his is an experience for everyone).

Stargirl by Jerry Spinelli. (Gr.6-9)
No middle-school teacher should go without reading this sweet treasure to his or her kids. Stargirl is a memorable girl who reminds us all of what individuality can and should be ... at home and at school.

Holes by Louis Sachar. (Gr.6-9)
I was so surprised to find that the author of the goofy Wayside School series (that I love to read aloud) wrote this gem. Middle school teachers, don't miss reading this story of a boy being sent to a most unusual reform camp for a crime he did not commit.

Mike Harte Was Here by Barbara Park. (Gr.4-8)
This is a must read for all middle school students. Barbara Park writes wonderfully funny books, but get out the tissues for this one. It is guaranteed to move you to tears.

Silverwing by Kenneth Oppel. (Gr.4-7)
A gripping fantasy about bats. Next to *Harry Potter*, *Silverwing* and *Sunwing* (the sequel) were the two most talked about books that I came across during my recent tour. I read them and loved them both. Two certain winners with this age group.

COLLECTIONS OF POETRY

A Child's Garden of Verses by Robert Louis Stevenson.
A classic. My wife would be cross with me if this title was not first on the list and she would have good reason to be. It is unsurpassed.

Now We Are Six by A.A. Milne.
Another classic and enormous fun to read aloud. Along the lines and almost as delightful as Stevenson's *Garden of Verses*. Some would argue that it is better than Stevenson's. This is another must on both Vicki's and my lists of five favorites. Try *When We Were Very Young* as well.

Poetry for Young People. (Gr.3-Adult)
This series is the best introduction that I've found to over a dozen classic poets. Each book includes a superb biography of one poet accompanied by excellent samples of his or her writings. Wonderfully illustrated. I recommend that you start with Henry Longfellow.

Revolting Rhymes by Roald Dahl. (Gr.2-10)
What can you say about Roald Dahl? He's been banned from numerous libraries for offending one group or another. Toronto's public library accused him of ageism in *George's Marvelous Medicine*. Few writers appeal more to reluctant readers than does Dahl. I particularly enjoy his *Revolting Rhymes* (probably because I wish I'd written them).

'Til All the Stars Have Fallen, selected by David Booth. Illustrated by Kady Macdonald Denton. (Gr.2-6)
A wonderful collection of diverse poems that span the twentieth century as well as Canada, coast to coast.

★ As a bonus, try *Then and Now* by Canadian storyteller and author Richard Thompson. This collection of poetry for young children is lovely to read and sure to generate thought and discussion.

COLLECTIONS AND SERIES

The Oxford Book of Modern Fairy Tales. (K-8)
Oxford Press does a number of wonderful books, but this is my favorite. I particularly appreciate its message to girls. You might care to start with "The Princess Who Stood on Her Own Two Feet." *Scarytales* is a similar anthology, well worth your attention.

The Magician's House Quartet by W. Corlett. (Gr.4-adult)
I have told every child and every parent for miles around how delightful this series is. The author is British and her stories are sure to captivate every reader.

The Magic Circle by Donna Jo Napoli. (Gr.6-10)
This book is one of a series that Napoli has based on popular fairy tales including "Hansel and Gretel," "Rapunzel," "The Frog Prince." In each case she chooses a new point of view. *The Magic Circle* is told from the point of view of the witch. Wonderfully woven stories, sure to hook you.

Junie B. Jones by Barbara Park. (K-Gr.8)
Had I not discovered my grade nine step-daughter in hysterics after reading one from this series, I'd have recommended it for K to 4. This middle-schooler called it the funniest book she had ever read. The series is a must if you read aloud to children.

The Fairy Tales of Oscar Wilde, illustrated by Michael Hague. (K-12)
No reading list of mine would be complete without something by Oscar Wilde. If there is any author whose style and spirit I would like to emulate, it is Oscar Wilde. This beautifully illustrated collection makes a beautiful gift for any child and a perfect read-aloud for everyone!

A SELECTION OF WENDY'S
FAVORITE BOOKS FOR READING ALOUD
(ALPHABETICAL BY AUTHOR)

PICTURE STORYBOOKS

Duck in the Truck, written and illustrated by Jez Alborough. (Gr.1-4)
The story of Duck's truck getting stuck in muck and the many
attempts of various animals to help him get unstuck is told in
simple language with clever internal rhyme and humor. Children will enjoy the author's bright, full-page illustrations and
the unexpected ending.

Cat, You Better Come Home by Garrison Keillor. Paintings by
Steve Johnson and Lou Fancher. (Gr.3-7)
In this narrative poem Keillor, who is known for his folksy story-
telling, laments the loss of his elegant cat Puff who has run away
from home to seek fame and fortune in Europe. The exaggeration
and humor used to tell the tale coupled with the bold, full-page
illustrations guarantee many requests to read it again.

The Elephant's Child by Rudyard Kipling. Illustrated by Leonard
Weisgard. (Gr.1-7)
One of Kipling's best known "Just So" stories, this story of how
the baby elephant got his long nose because of his "satiable
curtiosity" is a delight to read aloud. Weisgard's exquisite paintings of the jungle animals are large, vivid and full of action.

17 Kings and 42 Elephants by Margaret Mahy. Illustrated by
Patricia MacCarthy. (Gr.1-4)
Mahy is magical with words. This poem with its strong rhythm,
rhyme, and imaginative wordplay offers a rich language and

sound experience. "Umbrellaphants," "hippopotomums," and "rockodiles" are among the colorful animals watching the kings' "journey through a wild wet night."

Crocodile Crocodile by Peter Nickl and Binette Schroeder. (Gr.1-7)
Great fun to read aloud to any audience, this narrative poem about a crocodile sailing from the Nile to France to discover what is in the "crocodile store" is humorously supported by full-page, sophisticated illustrations.

The Travelling Musicians, retold by P.K. Page. Illustrated by Kady MacDonald Denton. (Gr.1-5)
Page's retelling of the Brothers Grimm folktale is uniquely fresh with appealing characterization and humor. The watercolor illustrations of the amusing, action-filled antics of the four music-loving animal friends perfectly complement the wit and charm of the text. A delight to read aloud.

Piggie Pie! by Margie Palatini. Illustrated by Howard Fine. (Gr.1-4)
The witty and creative language play in this twisting of a traditional fairy tale, combined with the bold, detailed illustrations, makes this a perfect book to read aloud. Children will join in the fun as Gritch the Witch is thwarted by the crafty barnyard animals in her search for a delicious treat.

Don't Fidget a Feather! by Erica Silverman. Illustrated by S.D. Schindler. (Gr.1-3)
Duck and Gander are always competing. One day as they are having a freeze-in-place contest, each determined to be the champion despite a host of distractions, a fox appears on the scene. Whimsically illustrated with pastels, the story grows more and more suspenseful until it reaches its satisfying conclusion.

The Camel Who Took a Walk by Jack Tworkov. Illustrated by Roger Duvoisin. (Gr.1-4)
The text of this cumulative tale makes it the perfect book to read aloud — it speaks directly to the listener as if in conversation, and has rich language, imagery, suspense, effective repetition, and humor. A personal favorite that I love to share.

Weighing the Elephant by Ting-xing Ye. Illustrated by Suzane
Langlois. (Gr.1-4)

In the green mountains of China a greedy emperor agrees to
return a baby elephant to the villagers if someone can tell him
how heavy it is. After many failed attempts by others, a young
boy outwits the emperor by solving the problem. The detailed
illustrations are stunning and complement the beautifully
written text.

Duffy and the Devil, retold by Harve Zemach. Illustrated by
Margot Zemach. (Gr.3-6)

Let listeners discover for themselves that this Cornish tale is a
version of the Rumplestiltskin story! The text is so full of
rollicking language, internal rhyme and conversation that it will
pick you up and carry you along. The illustrations are as
humorous and robust as the story.

NOVELS

Griffin & Sabine: An Extraordinary Correspondence by Nick
Bantock. (Gr.7-10)

While this multi-media art experience may not seem like a
novel, it has all the elements to classify as one. Older students
find it fascinating; some even emulate its structure, a series of
letters that the reader removes from their envelopes. This
trilogy, including *Sabine's Notebook* and *The Golden Mean*, is
an "extraordinary correspondence" that compels readers to
move with anticipation from each card or letter to the next. As
it progresses, the mystery deepens and the characters evolve.

Strange Objects by Gary Crew. (Gr.9-12)

Reading aloud gives teachers and parents an opportunity to
introduce innovative narrative structures. On an overnight school
trip, Stephen Messenger discovers artifacts from a seventeenth-
century shipwreck; clippings, articles, personal notes and entries
from a murderer's diary interweave to reveal the drama surrounding the ship's survivors and Stephen's connection to them. Even

my university students were fascinated with this novel and
compelled to reread it.

Cold Mountain by Charles Frazier. (Gr. 10-12)

By the senior grades, students are ready to hear many adult
novels read aloud. *Cold Mountain* is certainly one of them.
Journeys have been the subject of stories since time began. In
this novel Frazier, drawing upon his family history, details the
parallel journeys of two appealing characters who eventually are
reunited. Inman is a wounded, disillusioned Confederate soldier
who turns his back on the war and begins the long trek to his
home in the Blue Ridge Mountains. Ada, the woman he loves,
is experiencing her own personal journey towards self-knowl-
edge. Fascinating and satisfying.

Broken Ground by Jack Hodgins. (Gr. 10-12)

This complex novel, set after the First World War and presented in
three sections, is so skillfully written that the reader is guided
effortlessly through its narrative intricacies. Eleven narrators
introduce us to a pioneering community of war veterans who are
struggling to deal with soul-destroying challenges, personal
tensions and the tragedies caused by a forest fire. Part Two shifts to
France in 1918-1919 where the horrors of the war are revealed
through a series of letters. In the final section, set in 1996, one of
the original settlers narrates the events that took place in the
community immediately after the devastating fire. Older students'
literary experience will be richly broadened and many will look
forward to reading other equally challenging novels.

The Iron Man by Ted Hughes. (Gr.3+)

Originally titled *The Iron Giant: A Children's Story in Five Nights*,
England's poet laureate Hughes' story was written to be read
aloud. Its wealth of allegory makes it suitable for older readers,
while its rhythmic, precise language and sense of mystery and
adventure make it "work" on any level. I have given this book
to many beginning teachers, knowing that it will appeal to
most grade levels.

The Root Cellar by Janet Lunn. (Gr.4-8)

Having loved and recommended this book for many years, I was delighted when it was reissued in 1994, guaranteeing a new, enthusiastic readership. In this time-shift fantasy, Lunn skillfully balances a young girl's lonely life with a happier one in a previous century. Rose learns to step into the past through a root cellar door and there makes friends with Will and Susan. When Will fails to return from the American Civil War, the two girls set out to find him and soon become aware of the terrible cost of war.

A Little Lower Than the Angels by Geraldine McCaughrean. (Gr.5-7)

McCaughrean is such an outstanding writer for children that it was difficult to decide which book to select. Its fascinating glimpse of life in the Middle Ages, superb characterization and unusual experiences make this an ideal book to read to upper elementary children. Miserable as a stonemason apprentice, Gabriel escapes his cruel master by joining a troupe of mystery players and enters a life filled with illusion and unpredictable adventures.

Dog Friday by Hilary McKay. (Gr.3-7)

This is one of the funniest books I have read and great fun to share. The story focuses on ten-year-old Robin Brogan who, through a series of touching events, overcomes his fear of dogs. However, the marvelous humor lies in the contrast between the detached, third-person narration and the high-spirited dialogue and wild, creative antics of the Robinson children who become Robin's neighbors. Children will be eager to read more about the Robinsons in *The Amber Cat* and *Dolphin Luck*.

The Orphan Train Quartet by Joan Lowery Nixon. (Gr.6-8)

Nixon wrote *A Family Apart*, the first of this extremely popular series, after learning that between 1854 and 1929 the Children's Aid Society of New York City sent over a hundred thousand children west on the "orphan trains" to be adopted. Drawing upon this historical event, the four novels chronicle the lives of the six Kelly children after their widowed mother, unable to provide for them, puts them on a train going west from New

York City in the hopes that they will end up with families who will care for them. The courage of the children and their loyalty to one another help them survive as they face abandonment, abuse and separation. Once "hooked," children can hardly wait to read the other books in the quartet: *Caught in the Act, In the Face of Danger*, and *A Place to Belong*. Nixon is continuing the story of the Kelly family as they enter their teens in a new series, *The Orphan Train Adventures*.

The Golden Compass by Philip Pullman. (Gr.6-10)
In this first novel of his epic fantasy trilogy, *His Dark Materials*, Pullman creates a fully developed, alternate world, parallel to our own but different in many fascinating ways. After her best friend Roger becomes one of the children who have been mysteriously disappearing from an Oxford college, Lyra sets out for the Far North with her animal-like daemon to save the kidnapped children and their families from being subjected to gruesome experiments. Pullman is an extraordinarily fine writer and young people will be eager to read the other books in the trilogy, *The Subtle Knife* and *The Amber Spyglass*. His historical novel *The Ruby and the Smoke* is also a winner.

COLLECTIONS OF POETRY

The Earth Is Painted Green: A Garden of Poems about Our Planet, edited by Barbara Brenner. Illustrated by S.D. Schindler. (Gr.3-7)
Schindler's rich watercolors beautifully enhance this celebration of the diverse nature of our planet through ninety-one poems. This valuable anthology will help bring poetry into many areas of the elementary curriculum.

Peacock Pie: A Book of Rhymes by Walter de la Mare. (Gr.3-7)
De la Mare was regarded as the primary poet for children during the first half of the twentieth century; his insightful, rhythmic poems continue to be enjoyed today. Happily this collection, first published in 1913, was reissued in 1989 and is guaranteed to win an appreciative new audience if read aloud as

the topics will still have appeal for today's children. The beautiful poem "Silver" would be a fine place to begin.

Demi's Secret Garden, compiled and illustrated by Demi. (Gr.4-7+)
This exquisite collection is a treat for the ears and the eyes. Demi uses her trademark gold to embellish her stunning collages and intricately detailed illustrations, many opening into three- and four-page spreads. The poems she has chosen to describe the garden's small creatures include classic writers such as Shakespeare, Blake, Keats and Basho. Useful information on each insect is presented at the end of the book.

Words with Wrinkled Knees: Animal Poems by Barbara Esbensen. Illustrated by John Stadler. (Gr.3-7+)
This collection of twenty-one uniquely creative poems is one of my greatest favorites and one that I have enjoyed sharing for many years. Each poem plays with the sound of the animal's name, its nature and as a word itself — words-as-animals-as-words. The animal in the title, the elephant, "a lumbering gray word ... a word with wrinkled knees" or the bat that "all day hangs upside-down in the card catalog under B" are just two of the animals you will enjoy meeting in these free verse poems and sophisticated black-and-white illustrations.

Dogs & Dragons, Trees & Dreams by Karla Kuskin. (Gr.1-3)
A wonderfully prolific poet for young children, Kuskin incorporates into her poems the language qualities that appeal to them most — "words in their infinite color, length, shape, rhythm and, at times, rhyme." Although a number of her more than twenty-five collections are out of print, I was delighted that this collection, with Kuskin's insightful comments about poetry, was reissued in 1992. *Near the Window Tree*, another of my favorites, is well-worth looking for in the library.

The Pelican Chorus and Other Nonsense by Edward Lear. Illustrated by Fred Marcellino. (Gr.3-7)
With delightful playfulness, imagination, alliteration and rhythmic patterns, Lear's limericks and story poems appeal to children today as much as they did over a century ago. Never didactic, he

remains our foremost nonsense poet whose only goal was to entertain. Marcellino's light-hearted, lavish illustrations are great fun and perfectly complement the three story-poems in this collection: "The New Vestments," "The Owl and the Pussycat," and "The Pelican Chorus." The minute you see this book you will want to share it. Also treat your children to Marcellino's *I, Crocodile.*

A Crack in the Clouds and Other Poems by Constance Levy. Illustrated by Robin Bell Cornfield. (Gr.1-5)
Although this is only her fourth book, Levy has received enthusiastic praise for each of her collections. Her distinct voice, surprising insights, and sensitivity to a special magic in everyday things — snow, icicles, worms, whales, sunsets and fireworks — make her poems a pleasure to share.

I Never Did That Before by Lilian Moore. Illustrated by Lillian Hoban. (K-Gr.1)
These fourteen childlike poems celebrate moments young children experience for the very first time: holding a kitten; wearing new sneakers; overcoming fear of the dark, "He knows I'm too big now to scare"; and outgrowing one's clothes, "'Coat,' I explained, 'I grew.'" Hoban's illustrations include children of different cultures and capture the soft tone of Moore's gentle, rhyming verses. Treat yourself as well to Moore's delightful poetic prose in her book *I'll Meet You at the Cucumbers*, a winner with all who have read it.

Advice for a Frog by Alice Schertle. Illustrated by Norman Green. (Gr.3-6)
Accompanied by dramatic, lush illustrations, these poems sensitively describe some of the little known aspects of fourteen exotic animals from around the world. Both Schertle and Green have a deep respect and love for nature and for animals adding a poignant quality to the collection. Interesting information about each animal is provided at the end of the book.

All These Small Poems and Fourteen More by Valerie Worth.
   Illustrated by Natalie Babbitt. (Gr.3-7+)
   This important, hardcover edition is a wonderful compilation of
   all of Worth's ninety-nine beautifully crafted poems from earlier
   collections, plus fourteen new poems written shortly before her
   untimely death in 1994. Be it about porches or pigs, libraries
   or lawnmowers, garage sales or giraffes, each of Worth's
   poems leaves you with a fresh perspective and pleasure. If I
   could select only one poetry collection to share with young
   people, this would be it.

STORY COLLECTIONS

Eric Carle's Treasury of Classic Stories for Children, selected, retold ·
   and illustrated by Eric Carle. (Gr.1-6)
   This collection offers twenty-two of the folk and fairy tales, Aesop
   fables and wonderful stories of Hans Christian Andersen that
   adults love to share with children and children love to hear. Eric
   Carle has remained true to the original stories. His abundant,
   fanciful, unique illustrations make this a collection to treasure.

Eight Plus One, stories by Robert Cormier. (Gr.8-12)
   Well-respected for his strong, honest writing for adolescents (*I
   Am the Cheese* with its complex narrative structure is one of my
   favorites), Cormier reveals a gentler, more personal side in this
   collection as he shares stories written while he and his wife were
   raising three teenagers. Each story and the author comments
   that accompany it reflect his skill and sensitivity as a writer and
   his understanding of the challenges young people face.

Diane Goode's Book of Scary Stories and Songs, compiled and
   illustrated by Diane Goode. (Gr.1-4)
   Gentle enough for early primary, these seventeen folk tales from
   various cultures around the world will excite and delight rather
   than frighten young children. Goode explains that scary stories
   about ghosts and goblins help us overcome our fear; her soft,
   pastel illustrations support this claim.

In the Beginning: Creation Stories from Around the World, told by
Virginia Hamilton. Illustrated by Barry Moser. (Gr.4-8)
A deserving winner of many awards, this outstanding collection
of twenty-five creation myths is enriched by Moser's stunning
works of art. Through these myths from cultures as diverse as
those of India, Greece, and Nigeria, readers gain insight into
the varied beliefs explaining the beginning of humankind.
Research for both the art and text was extensive and at the end
of each story Hamilton comments on its origin and interpretation. A valuable collection that will encourage further inquiry.

Frederick's Fables: A Leo Lionni Treasury of Favorite Stories by
Leo Lionni. (Gr.1-4+)
This compilation of thirteen of Lionni's picture books is a
treasure. Each of the animal fables, ***Frederick*** and ***Swimmy***
being my all-time favorites, is unabridged and accompanied by
a number of the original illustrations. A lengthy introduction
by Bruno Bettelheim provides valuable insight into Lionni's
work and its universal appeal for children. A "must have" for
anyone associated with children.

A Professional Bibliography

Barron, Marlene. *I Learn to Read and Write the Way I Learn to Talk*. Richard C. Owen, 1990.

Bergeron. B.S. "What does the term whole language mean? Constructing a definition from the literature." In *Journal of Reading Behaviour*. 22, 4, 301-329, 1990.

Bialostok, Steven. *Raising Readers: Helping Your Child to Literacy*. Peguis, 1992.

Booth, David. *Guiding the Reading Process: Techniques and Strategies for Successful Instruction in K-8 Classrooms*. Stenhouse, 2000. (reissued)

Carlsen, Robert G. and Anne Sherrill. *Voices of Readers: How We Come To Love Books*. National Council of Teachers of English (NCTE), 1988.

Chambers, Aidan. *The Reading Environment: How adults help children enjoy books*. Thimble Press, 1991.

Chukovsky, Kornei. *From Two to Five*. University of California Press, 1974/ 1925 in Russian.

Clay, Marie M. *An Observation Survey of Literacy Achievement*. Heinemann, 1993.

Cochrane, Orin. *Questions and Answers about Whole Language*. Richard C. Owen, 1992.

Cochrane, Orin and Donna, et al. *Reading, Writing and Caring*. Richard C. Owen, 1984.

Cullinan, Bernice. *Let's Read About Finding Books They'll Love to Read*. Scholastic, 1993.

Cullinan, Bernice E. *Read To Me: Raising Kids Who Love to Read*. Scholastic, 2000 (1992).

Froese, Victor, ed. *Whole Language: Practice and Theory*, 2nd ed. Allyn & Bacon, 1996.

Goodlad, John. *The Nongraded Elementary School*. Teachers College Press, 1987 (1959).

Goodman, Vera. *Reading Is More Than Phonics!* Reading Circles, 1996.

Heald-Taylor, Gail. *The Administrator's Guide to Whole Language*. Richard C. Owen, 1989.

Hiebert, E.H. *Literacy for a Diverse Society: Perspectives, practices, and policies*. Teachers College Press, 1991.

Hurst, Otis. *Long Ago and Far Away*. DLM, 1991.

Kohn, Alfred. *The Schools Our Children Deserve*. Houghton Mifflin, 1999.

Krashen, Stephen. *The Power of Reading: Insights from the Research*. Libraries Unlimited, 1993.

Kropp, Paul. *The Reading Solution: Make Your Child a Reader for Life*. Random House, 1993.

Langer, Judith A. *Envisioning Literature: Literary Understanding and Literature Instruction*. Teachers College, Columbia University, 1995.

Lipson, Eden Ross. *The* New York Times *Parents' Guide to the Best Books for Children*. Random House, 1991.

Meek, Margaret. *On Being Literate*. Heinemann, 1992 (Bodley Head, 1991). Also: *How Texts Teach What Readers Learn*. Thimble Press, 1988.

Nell, Victor. *Lost in a Book: The Psychology of Reading for Pleasure*. Yale University Press, 1988.

Tierney, Robert J. *Reading Strategies and Practices: A Compendium, 5th ed.* Allyn & Bacon, 2000.

Tompkins, Gail E. and Lea M. McGee. *Teaching Reading with Literature: Case Studies to Action Plans*. Merrill, an imprint of Macmillan Pub. Co., 1993.

Trelease, Jim. *The Read-Aloud Handbook*. Penguin, 1995.

DAVID BOUCHARD has been a tireless champion of literacy for many years. A non-reader until adulthood, he fell in love with children's books one day when he was asked to read aloud to an eighth grade class. He has now retired from his long, successful career as a teacher and school-based administrator to devote his time to writing and to promoting reading. He has won many awards for his writing for children. His popular titles include *Prairie Born, A Barnyard Bestiary* and his new picture book, *Fairy*.

WENDY SUTTON, professor emerita, taught both elementary and secondary school before joining the Department of Language and Literacy Education at the University of British Columbia where she was awarded the University Excellence in Teaching Prize. A well-respected presenter at conferences in Canada, the US and Great Britain, Wendy chaired many major committees as a member of the National Council of Teachers of English. Still active at the university, she is now retired and serves as a language arts/children's literature consultant.